Come to the
QUIET

Come to the
QUIET

DENISE GEORGE

BETHANYHOUSE
Minneapolis, Minnesota

Published by Bethany House Publishers
11400 Hampshire Avenue South
Bloomington, Minnesota 55438
www.bethanyhouse.com

Bethany House Publishers is a Division of
Baker Book House Company, Grand Rapids, Michigan.

Printed in the United States of America

Library of Congress Cataloging-in-Publication Data

George, Denise.
    Come to the quiet : the secrets of solitude and rest / by Denise George.
       p. cm.
Includes bibliographical references.
    ISBN 0-7642-2658-4 (pbk.)
    1. Christian women—Religious life. 2. Rest—Religious aspects—Christianity.
I. Title.
BV4527.G454   2003
248.8'43—dc21   2003000976

DEDICATION

For Oscar S. Hilliard

With deep admiration and much love ,

DENISE GEORGE is a frequent speaker in many locations around the world and the author of more than a dozen books, including *God's Heart, God's Hands* and *Kids Can Talk to God*, as well as over 1,200 articles. She and her husband, Timothy George, Founding Dean of Beeson Divinity School, Samford University, Birmingham, Alabama, are the parents of two grown children.

Contents

Jesus said:

"Come to Me, all you who labor
and are heavy laden,
and I will give you rest."

(Matthew 11:28 NKJV)

Rest

*I*NTRODUCTION

EXHAUSTION AND THE
TWENTY-FIRST-CENTURY WOMAN

I meet women every day—in every walk of life, in every age group, with children and without children, who work inside and/or outside the home—who are mentally exhausted, physically depleted, and emotionally/spiritually drained.

No doubt you meet them too. You may, in fact, be one of them. If so, I have written this book especially for you.

Exhaustion has become the new look of the twenty-first-century woman.

As you already know, our present society is restless. We can look into the average woman's eyes and see her weariness. We can look into a mirror and see our own weariness. Women today generally have too many responsibilities to manage, too many jobs to handle, and too many demands on our already over-worked bodies. Stress, worry, guilt, and society's anxieties can play havoc with our emotions.

Some of us teeter on the brink of spiritual disaster, for we have given ourselves too little, if any, time to mend, nurture, and replenish our dry souls. Let me ask you a few questions. When was the last time you stopped on a warm summer morning and breathed in the fragrance of freshly mowed grass? When was the last time you sat down just to listen to spring's raindrops tap against your window? How long has it been since you had a quiet moment to refresh yourself with a cup of herbal tea or other refreshing drink? Or shared a dinner with a friend "just for fun"?

Or read a book of fiction from cover to cover in one sitting? Or fished on the bank of a river on a peaceful afternoon?

Can't remember? Then read this book carefully, and listen to the One who loves you and who calls you to come to Him and rest.

In response to my question, most women honestly answer, "It's been a long time since I've rested." For many women, "rest" is that unexpected and unscheduled white space on their daily calendars. They allow themselves to rest only when they've not planned something else to do, or when no one else has planned something for them to do. I truly believe that the average woman today has never learned how to rest, nor does she understand the tremendous value of rest. Have you discovered the treasure of a restful moment? Have you discovered the healing of a deep plunge into the Quiet?

Maybe you, like women I meet day after day, mistakenly define "rest" as "a one-hour collapse in the middle of an exhausting week." Or "a family supper at a restaurant once or twice a month." Or "a thirty-minute extra sleep-in on Saturday morning." While these are "rests" of a sort, they are not those soul-satisfying, deeply spiritual moments of peaceful rest and renewal spent in the Quiet Place with the One who so dearly loves you.

Throughout the pages of this book, I want to personally introduce you to the Quiet Place. I believe that we, as women, need deep, relaxing, satisfying, and nurturing rest. Scheduled and regular rest.

We need times of solitude. Often.

We need rest for our exhausted *minds,* minds that must constantly keep up with complicated schedules, minds that are stretched to their limits with increasing demands and responsibilities.

We need rest for our tired *bodies,* bodies that work far too hard and run in too many different directions.

We need rest for our weary *souls,* souls that are weighed down with stress and pain and worry and guilt. Spirits whose vessels have run dry and need to be filled up to the brim with fresh Living Water.[1]

I know of few women these days, however, who plan purposeful rest and solitude for their mental, physical, or spiritual health and well-being. Some complain, "I don't have time to rest." Others tell me, "I have too many people depending on me. I have too many responsibilities to rest." A few women have even confessed: "I feel *guilty* when I stop to rest. I might hurt someone's feelings if I ask for solitude!"

Over the years I have discovered that if a woman doesn't take time to rest—mentally, physically, and spiritually—she will soon register "empty" and break down. Maybe you have already registered "empty." Just as our cars require gasoline to run, we need a "tank" full of rest if we are to complete the journey God has called us to travel. If we don't incorporate rest into our daily schedule, we will end up wrecked somewhere along life's roadside. We will join the other tired and empty women who were unable to continue. Throughout the ages women have driven themselves into "dis-ease" and even death simply because they would not take the time to stop and rest.

Dear friend: *Rest is not a luxury. Rest is a necessity.* We need regular rest in order to maintain ourselves as whole, healthy women!

Rest comes in three parts, and we need each part in our lives in order to function as God intended: We need mental rest, physical rest, and spiritual rest. God made our minds, bodies, and souls to require regular, purposeful rest. He offers us the gift of rest as well as the gift of himself in the place called "Quiet." Jesus invites us, calls us, urges us to "Come to the Quiet" to be with Him.

A few weeks ago I had a conversation about the virtues of rest with a middle-aged woman (a wife, mother, and grandmother) who works too hard and juggles far too many responsibilities. She laughed and told me, "I don't have the luxury of rest in my life!"

"Do you consider rest a *luxury*?" I asked her. "I consider rest a *necessity*, an investment in my future and my family's future."

She fished her large Bible from an overstuffed canvas bag and opened it to Proverbs 31.

"Do you see this woman?" she asked me, pointing to verse 10. "This woman didn't rest! She worked with 'eager hands, got up while it was still dark, brought her family's food from afar, and set about her work vigorously with strong arms.' Do you see anything in this passage about stopping to rest?"

Before I could challenge her, she continued, "This Proverbs 31 woman buys and sells real estate, plants vineyards, weaves and sews and cooks! She never stops! And her husband and children call her *blessed* because of all her hard work."

My friend stepped back, smiled, and nervously tapped her foot.

She was right! The Proverbs 31 woman was Superwoman, a hard worker who loved God and her family. She seemed to toil nonstop from before dawn to long after dark.

However, my friend had failed to reflect on verse 26, where Scripture tells us that this industrious woman "speaks with *wisdom*, and *faithful instruction* is on her tongue" (emphasis mine).

Yes, "her life was beautiful and [she] touched everyone around her in a positive way. Because she placed the Lord first, she was balanced in everything else."[2]

The Proverbs 31 woman provides an extraordinary example for us today not only because of her hard work but also for the incredible amount of godly *wisdom* she held in her heart and on her tongue.

Throughout Scripture we are told that *wisdom*, understanding, and *faithful instruction* come from God.

For instance, the psalmist states, "The fear of the Lord is the beginning of wisdom; all who follow His precepts have good understanding" (Psalm 111:10). The Proverbs 31 woman feared the Lord (see verse 31), making her worth immeasurable: "Choose my instruction instead of silver, knowledge rather than choice gold, for wisdom is more precious than rubies, and nothing you desire can compare with her" (8:10–11).

James 1:5 tells us, "If any of you lacks wisdom, he should ask God, who gives generously to all." The Proverbs 31 woman was a wise woman first and a hardworking woman second. Her heavenly wisdom made her "worth far more than rubies," as James 3:17 proves: "The wisdom that comes from heaven is first of all pure; then peace-loving, considerate, submissive, full of mercy and good fruit, impartial and sincere."

Wisdom comes from the Lord. What we aren't told is that this woman of wisdom spent considerable time *away from her work* and within the restful arms of God's instruction. Surely it was during those quiet times of rest and solitude that she received her God-given wisdom; without her wisdom, her work would have had little value. Had she been ill or physically disabled or elderly or incapable of work, I believe her God-granted wisdom alone would have brought her ample praise from her husband and children. She is uniquely valuable to God and her family because of her wisdom—not just because of her work.

Should you and I feel guilty when we stop our work and rest? Of course not! Taking a rest is not wasting time or being lazy. Resting our mind, body, and soul is a priceless investment in our future and in the lives of those we love. You and I must learn to rest regularly.

> [We must learn the] importance of divinely appointed rest. . . . Rest [that] offers an opportunity to reflect on the Lord and what He has done for you. [Rest that] gives you time to recharge your own batteries—to be filled so that you can empty yourself again in kingdom ministries.[3]

God made us with a built-in need to rest! Jesus tells us to rest! When we learn *how* to rest, when we learn *why* we must rest, we also learn about the goal and glorious results of rest—the God-directed transformation of our mind, body, and soul. This precious gift of total revitalization, of divine wisdom, comes to us when we follow His Word, obey His commands, and find our rest in Him alone.

Let me ask you the question that I have asked myself many times: Why do we live such an "ironic existence, complaining about how tired and overwhelmed we feel, but refusing to accept the gift of rest God offers?"[4] Why do we resist our Lord's invitation when He urges us, "Come to Me . . . and I will give you rest"? Certainly you and I suffer severely when we fail to realize how important regular rest and solitude are.

Won't you stop right now and accept the gift of rest that God offers you? Won't you decide to experience the hope and peace that God will bring you through solitude and quiet? Ask God to direct you in purposeful rest and in so doing to transform you more closely to His image. Please come to the Quiet Place, where Jesus waits, learn the secrets of rest and solitude, and allow God to work a transforming miracle in your mind, body, and spirit.

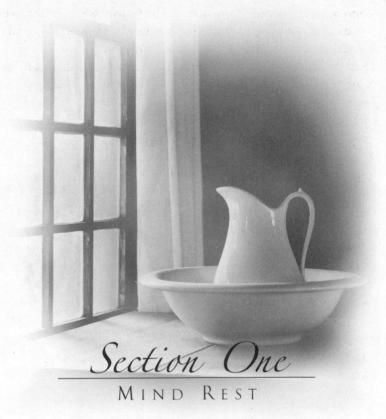

Section One

MIND REST

JESUS SAID: "COME TO ME . . ."
(MATTHEW 11:28 NKJV)

Chapter One

MAMA'S SHOULDER

The year was 1956. I was five years old. My mother, grand-mother, and I had been shopping, and I was exhausted. We had been in and out of all the busy stores that lined the length of Rossville Boulevard on that cool Saturday after-noon in northern Georgia. My young mind was whirling with all the frantic activity that surrounded us. We still had two more places to stop: Loveman's Department Store and Bon-Ton's Dress Shop. I was worn out, but my mother's shopping energy got a new burst when she saw the 75-percent-discount sale sign in Bon-Ton's window. That's when my wise grandmother, "Mama" (pronounced "MawMaw"), noticed my glazed-over eyes. She diagnosed correctly that I had a bad case of "shopper's shock." She took me by the hand, and said, "Come with me, 'Nisey," and led me away from the chaotic crowd.

"Willene," she called to my mother above the noise and din of shoppers. "You go into Bon-Ton's. 'Nisey and I will wait for you in the car."

I shall forever thank Mama for that brilliant suggestion! We forced our way against the flow of bargain-hunting humanity and escaped through the maze to my mother's large black Chevrolet. Once inside the comfortable interior, I breathed a sigh of relief. I had finally found a quiet place, a place of solitude, far from the hustle and bustle of salespeople and shoppers.

Tired and sleepy, I laid my head on my grandmother's shoulder. I felt her soft woolen coat against my face. I smelled the lingering vanilla flavoring she had spooned into that morning's pound cakes. I closed my eyes and listened to her breathing. I heard her reassuring words gently urging me, "Be still, precious one, and rest."

A storm of sorts brewed outside our car: a shower of shoppers; to my small ears, thunderous traffic and lightning bolts of sharp words shouted over parking spaces. Inside, however, Mama's shoulder provided a secure sanctuary of peace and rest.

I opened my eyes to disrupt my rest only once. From the car window, I saw shoppers hurrying in and out of the stores, lugging packages and bags. I watched white-gloved mothers tug at tired little girls who had sore feet stuffed into new patent leather shoes. I saw old women wearing high-heeled pumps and Sunday morning hats trying to keep up with the younger shoppers to grab up the best buys. I finally closed my eyes when I noticed the handful of bored husbands, suited up in starched white shirts, waiting together on Bon-Ton's benches and bemoaning their misery in irritated unison.

I closed my eyes and went to sleep. For the next few minutes, I left the world of crying kids and cosmic chaos—that simple slice of Americana we called Saturday shopping. Mama and I had purposely escaped the mayhem. We had stepped out of the confusing world and into the cocoon of rest.

I have treasured that brief snapshot of memory for more than forty-five years—it explains so well what I want to say in the pages of this book. Because just as my beloved grandmother offered me a haven of solitude and rest in the middle of a noisy crowd of Saturday shoppers, Jesus offers you and me a place of rest and refuge in the middle of a very busy society. He offers us His shoulder. Where there is disorder and unrest, we can lay our heads on Him, and find order and peace. It is a rest that will transform every part of our being.

Thomas á Kempis writes,

> The person who wants to arrive at interiority and spirituality has to leave the crowd behind and spend some time with Jesus. . . . Cultivate the solitude of your cell, and guard against the invasions of your quietude.[1]

What happens when you and I leave the crowds and spend time in the Quiet with Christ?

> In quiet and silence the faithful soul makes progress, the hidden meanings of the Scriptures become clear, and the eyes weep with devotion. . . . As one learns to grow still, he draws closer to the Creator and farther from the hurly-burly of the world.[2]

To that statement, I say, "Amen!" Are you ready to draw closer to the Creator? I am.

If so, "Shut the door behind you . . . [and] call Jesus, your beloved friend, to join you. Remain with him in your cell because you won't find such peace elsewhere."[3]

I have learned something significant about laying my head on Jesus' shoulder. Jesus offers us not just mental rest from the noise and chaos of the world, not just physical rest from the work and demands, not just soul rest from our worries and problems, but a deep invigorating rest in Him. The deeper rest He describes is a transforming rest. When you and I come to Him, when we ask Him to become Lord and Savior of our lives, He bestows on us a quiet rest not found anywhere else on earth. It is a peaceful rest that passes the world's understanding. When we remain in our "cell" with Him, He gives us Living Water to drink. He also readies heaven itself for our future arrival.

"In my Father's house are many rooms," Jesus tells His disciples. "If it were not so, I would have told you. I am going there to prepare a place for you" (John 14:2).

Inner peaceful rest, the rest that passes the world's understanding, comes only from knowing that He has prepared a room in heaven for you. You and I can claim deep satisfying rest because we know our future is in God's capable hands, and that He has promised us, His children, eternal life with Him. Forever.

Jesus made the offer clear enough for a child to understand. "Come to Me," He calls. "I am the way and the truth and the life. No one comes to the Father except through Me" (John 14:6). Surely the most significant rest we can possess is in knowing that God loves us and that we will spend eternity with Him. When you and I are assured of our destiny forever, we will find rest for our soul that is greater than any rest earth can offer.

GENUINE SOUL-REST

Genuine soul-rest is possible because we know that God loves us. I have no idea why He loves us, His human creation. Since Adam and Eve, we have continually disappointed our Creator. We have selfishly turned to our own way and rejected God's path for us. No human being is exempt from this crime.

"We come into this world created in God's image, but we also share in the consequences of humanity's fall from grace, in our natural propensity to sin."[4]

Because of our "natural propensity" to sin, we have moved far away from our God-image. For a time God removed His shoulder from the heads of Adam and Eve. God still loved His human creation, but He put a stop to those precious walks in the Garden with Him. Paradise was lost for Adam and Eve and for the rest of humanity. Fellowship became broken between the perfect Creator and His sinful creatures. What event did our Father orchestrate to enable us once again to know that deep satisfying soul-rest—eternal life with Him?

He sent to us His only Son, Jesus! The Scripture my grandfather, Papa ("PawPaw"), taught me years ago still brings awe to my heart and tears of gratitude to my eyes: "For God so loved the world that He gave His one and only Son, that whoever believes in Him shall not perish but have eternal life" (John 3:16).

Because God loved us, He made a way for us to come back to Him, even if it meant the death of His only Son. Now when God looks at you and me, His sinful creatures, He no longer sees us in our ugly sin. Instead, He sees His sinless Son, Jesus.

A restored relationship with God comes to us in the shape of a cross. God reached down to us through Jesus. Because Jesus died to restore this relationship with God, we can once again reach up to the Lord. Without the cross, we have no good news. Without the cross, we have a fractured family with no way of spending eternity with our Father. Transformation and healing happen only through the cross of Christ.

"Man is born broken," writes Eugene O'Neill. "He lives by mending. The grace of God is glue."[5]

Our present-day society, however, incorrectly believes that transformation and healing happen in contemporary therapy sessions.

> People today are ostensibly exposed to the transforming power of therapy. [They think] you arrive on earth perfect and good, then bad things happen to you, so now you are broken and in need of mending. The Christian message is just the opposite: You arrived here with a potentially fatal flaw, but by turning to Christ and handing your life over to Him (literally "dying to self" by replacing your wants and desires with His, instead of cultivating and healing your own self), you will be brought back into God's kingdom.[6]

WHY DOES GOD LOVE US?

Why does God love us? He doesn't have to. He owes us nothing, not even life. He doesn't need us—He is all-powerful and has perfect fellowship within His triune self. He wouldn't be lonely without us—He is complete.

Why does He love us? As I said before, I don't know why. I cannot even imagine an unconditional love as great as His. It is grace, and only grace.

> Grace means there is nothing I can do to make God love me more, and nothing I can do to make God love me less. It means that I, even I who deserve the opposite, am invited to take my place at the table in God's family.[7]

For my personal place at God's family table, I thank Him with every breath I breathe. *Thank you, Lord, that you love me, in spite of myself.* Certainly "the rediscovery of the precious gift of life and existence, often taken for granted, gives birth to the spirit of gratefulness!"[8]

Let me tell you about a creator who didn't love his creation. In fact, this creator intensely hated the creature he had made—he spent his lifetime trying to kill it. His name was Dr. Victor Frankenstein.

I recently rediscovered an old, unsettling book: Mary Shelley's *Frankenstein*. The original story of un-grace, written in 1816, deals with a human scientist who creates a devilish creature. The monster he forms is grotesquely horrible and commits a multitude of murders. The creator comes to despise the sinful, evil creature, seeking with his last breath to destroy him.

Can a creator hate his own creation? Can a "father" hate his own "child"? Dr. Victor Frankenstein did.

In the summer of 1816, a young woman, Mary Wollstonecraft, only nineteen years old, was spending the months with her lover, Percy Shelley. (Never mind that Percy Shelley had a wife and two children.) Mary and Percy lived that summer at the Villa Diodati, on the edge of Lake Geneva in Cologny, Switzerland, as houseguests of the infamous Lord Byron. Not long after, Percy's distraught wife, Harriet, drowned herself. Two weeks following, Mary and Percy would marry.

One dark rainy night, in the bowels of the lonely Villa Diodati, Lord Byron issued a dare to his bored guests. He dared them to each write a story—a ghost story. Mary Shelley's tale has survived almost two centuries.

The old movie *Frankenstein,* with actor Boris Karloff, is silly and seeks only to scare its viewers. It hardly reflects the deep spiritual struggle forced upon Dr. Victor Frankenstein and his monstrous creation.

Several years before 1816, scientists were beginning to experiment with electricity, using the newly discovered power in attempts to resuscitate drowning victims and to restore life to the recently dead. Often, in deep and fascinating conversations, Lord Byron and the Shelleys would discuss Luigi Galvani's earlier tests with electricity, called "galvanism." To create the monster, Mary Shelley had Victor Frankenstein "dabble among the unhallowed damps of the grave," frequent "dissecting rooms and slaughterhouses," and put together various body parts "from corpses and decaying tissue."[9] Needless to say, the author used the recently discovered, mysterious current of electricity to supply the monster's life force.

The Monster Frankenstein Hated

Dr. Frankenstein had done the impossible! He had created a creature, a living, breathing thing that resembled a human being. However, his creation was sinful and vile. His monster killed those people that the scientist most loved. When Dr. Frankenstein looked upon his murderous creation, he detested him. He speaks of the monster's "unearthly ugliness [that] rendered it almost too horrible for human eyes" and of his own "rage and hatred."

Upon meeting the creature, Dr. Frankenstein declares,

> Devil, do you dare approach me? And do not you fear the
> fierce vengeance of my arm wreaked on your miserable head?
> Begone, vile insect! Or rather, stay, that I may trample you to
> dust . . . abhorred monster! Fiend that thou art! The tortures
> of hell are too mild a vengeance for thy crimes. Wretched
> devil! You reproach me with your creation; come on, then,
> that I may extinguish the spark which I so negligently
> bestowed.[10]

Mary Shelley's readers, however, do not fear the "monster"
that Dr. Frankenstein considered "too horrible for human eyes"
and outrageously hated. Instead, they feel sorry for the unnamed
creature, for without his knowledge, the monster had been created and then abandoned. The father-creator should have loved
and protected his child-creation, no matter how hideous the
results, no matter how horrible his crimes. Instead, Dr. Frankenstein rejects him. Without the love of even his creator, he finds
himself alone and miserable.

The monster moans,

> Everywhere I see bliss from which I alone am irrevo-
> cably excluded. . . . I desired love and fellowship, and I
> was still spurned. . . . I, the miserable and the abandoned,
> am an abortion, to be spurned at, and kicked, and tram-
> pled on. . . . Even that enemy of God and man [Satan] had
> friends and associates in his desolation; I am alone.[11]

Who can conceive of a mother hating her own child? Who
can comprehend how Dr. Frankenstein could create a creature
and then abandon it? Mary Shelley's tragic story brings us back
to the unanswerable question: "Why does my Creator, Almighty
God, love me?"

> Throughout the Bible the central question is "How
> can sinful man ever be accepted by a holy God?" The

Bible takes sin seriously. . . . It sees sin as a barrier separating man from God (Isaiah 59:2), a barrier that man was able to erect but is quite unable to demolish. [Scripture] shows that it is the death of Christ and not any human achievement that brings salvation.[12]

VILE AND UGLY SIN

Are we not, in our own shocking state of sin, just as hideous and "wretched" to our Creator God as the created monster was to his creator, Dr. Frankenstein? When God, who is holy, looks upon us, His sinful creatures, why does He, like Dr. Frankenstein, not declare, "Devil, do you dare approach me? . . . Begone, vile insect! . . . The tortures of hell are too mild a vengeance for thy crimes"?

Why does God love us when we have made ourselves unlovable through vile and ugly sin? How can we have fellowship—deep, loving friendship—with a perfect God who detests sin?

You already know the answer—this is the amazing part of the Gospel story! God, our Creator, has made a way to restore the friendship with us, His sinful creatures. Unlike Victor Frankenstein, who bestows no forgiveness, whose creature finds no redemption and no grace, our Creator sent us a Redeemer and offers to forgive us of the "unearthly ugliness" that our sin has produced.

It was much, that man was made like God before
But, that God should be made like man, much more.[13]

Why did God create us? Did He *need* us? No!

"God, who needs nothing, loves into existence wholly superfluous creatures in order that He may love and perfect them," wrote C. S. Lewis.[14]

It's called "grace." Grace is a gift to us from God! It is when we experience repentance ("a feeling of regret, a changing of the mind, or a turning from sin to God") that we understand and treasure His grace.[15]

T. W. Hunt, and his daughter, Melana Hunt Monroe, write,

> God does not love His children because of our attrac-
> tiveness, or our service for Him, or our gifts to Him. He
> loves us because that is who He is! A new father loves his
> infant because of his identity as father, not because the
> baby has earned any love.[16]

We can be reconciled to God because He made Jesus, who had no sin, to *be* sin for us, so that in Him we might become the righteousness of God. When sin made us an "abhorred monster," and a perfect, holy Creator could not stand to look upon us, Jesus became "flesh," a human being, and gave His life to redeem us! This is the saving message Jesus preached and taught to the crowds that gathered around Him, the message He shouts to us today: "I have come that they may have life, and have it to the full" (John 10:10).

Through His death on the cross, Jesus took our hideousness onto himself. When God looks at us, He no longer sees us as sinful monsters "too horrible for human eyes." He sees His Son, Jesus, covering our awful ugliness. Jesus opens the way for us to reach up to God, our perfect Creator, the One who loves us, the One who saves us from eternal desolation, the One who calls us to himself for fellowship and rest. Because of Jesus, you and I can walk and talk with God once more. Because of Jesus, you and I can rest our tired heads on God's comforting shoulder. Without Jesus, genuine soul-rest is impossible.

Grace! Grace! Grace!

We can "take our place at the table in God's family" because Jesus laid down His life for you and me. "Greater love has no one than this," Jesus said, "that he lay down his life for his friends" (John 15:13). We deserved nothing; He gave us His all. For what He has done for us, we should be grateful servants, bowing down and kissing His feet. He surprises us even further when He tells us that we are *His friends* (John 15:15–16).

Friends?! The Creator and the sinful creature are friends?! How unspeakably fortunate we are that God has loved us enough to send Jesus to redeem us, to restore our precious fellowship with Him! Oh, how Frankenstein's lonely and unloved monster would have treasured those words from his creator!

OUR RESPONSE TO A LOVING FATHER

How should we respond to our Father's gift of eternal life and satisfying rest with Him? With thanksgiving and celebration! With prayer and meditation and contemplation of His love and mercy! With obedience to read and follow His Word! With mission minds, hearts, and hands that reach out with the good news of Jesus to others, telling them how they too can come back to the Father who loves them! We come with a plea to the Father to transform us, to draw us closer to himself, to make us like His Son, Jesus! With the heartfelt desire to come to the Quiet, we come to Christ. With sincere gratitude for His remarkable grace, and with a prayer in our hearts and a song on our lips, we can lay our weary head on His strong shoulder and there find rest.

Chapter Two

OUR MIND – CREATED FOR THE QUIET

O ur Creator gave us an incredible gift when He created our minds. D. Martyn Lloyd-Jones believes,

> According to the Scripture man was made in the image of God; and a part of the image of God in man is undoubtedly the *mind*, the ability to think and to reason, especially in the highest sense and in a spiritual sense.[1]

I believe that the One who created us, the God who loves us, made our minds to think and to reason and to relate to Him, and also to need rest.

Several years ago I learned this lesson the hard way. I became mentally overwhelmed by the work of the world. Working outside the home, raising two preschoolers, maintaining a house, and keeping up with the family's finances, I found myself mentally tired and unable to concentrate. I desperately needed to "escape" from the noise and pressure and work of family and society. My soul yearned for a retreat. My body longed for a few days of solitude and simple rest. My mind craved a visit to the Quiet, far away from the ever-busy pace of life. I desperately needed to sit still and listen to God's gentle whisper, to meditate, to cleanse my body and soul of sound, everyday demands, and hectic confusion. I was desperate for a rest. I felt like King David when he cried out for the wings of a bird that he might fly away and find rest.

> My thoughts trouble me and I am distraught. . . . My heart is in anguish within me. . . . Oh, that I had *the wings of a dove!* I would fly away and be at rest—I would flee far away. . . . I would hurry to my place of shelter, far from the tempest and storm. (Psalm 55:2–8, emphasis mine)

Fortunately my husband's work schedule allowed him to take over everything at home for a few days so that I could get away. At the time, Timothy and I were taking a teaching sabbatical in Switzerland. With his blessing, I packed a few clothes and traveled to the quietest place on earth—Kappal.

A MOUNTAINTOP IN SWITZERLAND

I arrived in Kappal, a Swiss canton resting high upon the top of a mountain, late one October afternoon. For the next three days I found pure, deep, restful solitude along with some early first snows. I touched the snow-dusted baby pines that looked like they had been sprinkled with powdered sugar. I spent my mornings walking, feeling gentle snowflakes brush my face, and breathing in the fresh mountain air. In the afternoons, I retraced the footsteps of Huldrych (Ulrich) Zwingli, the great Protestant reformer who fought at Kappal and died in battle on the grounds beneath my feet. All was quiet and lonely and lovely. The battle sounds of half a millennium ago had long diminished. It was now a place of no confusion, no demands, and no interruptions.

Resident nuns gave me a small, warm room in the twelfth-century stone monastery that perched on the mountain's top and reached up into the clouds. High above the world's bustling humanity, I walked the old dirt paths made millennia before by peasants bringing produce down to the villages to sell. A few elderly nuns still lived at the monastery, but they didn't speak English, and I didn't speak German. A simple smile communicated our mutual love for the Lord and for His beautiful creation at Kappal.

I spent wonderful days outside, wandering through snow-covered meadows, drinking in unimaginable beauty, enjoying soft breezes. I felt contented beyond words there in the Quiet. I communed only with God. In the early mornings, I stroked the heads of a few brown and white cows that slowly chewed their cud. I spent my nights on a tiny cozy cot, piled high with antique quilts. I felt warm and safe within the thick stone walls.

I rested in the Quiet all night, every night. An occasional moo of a Swiss cow was the only sound that interrupted the welcomed silence. I lay in bed and imagined medieval monks of centuries past, moving through the halls on their way to midnight mass. I slept wrapped in rest, quilts, and precious peace. My overworked mind snuggled with solitude.

During those days I walked, I slept, and I prayed long uninterrupted prayers of confession, thanksgiving, adoration, and petition. It was as if I saw the world with new eyes. I heard rare sounds with new ears. I breathed deeply the refreshing mountain air. I stuck out my tongue and caught and tasted the gently falling snowflakes. My mind tingled within me in new excitement and keener concentration.

I walked with God on that tall Swiss mountain. I treasured every second of solitude with Him. Surrounded by quiet, I heard every small sound of the Creator's creation. I listened to it intently, as if I had spent my lifetime before without ears. The birds sang, the cows chewed, an occasional hedgehog shuffled through the new dusting of snow.

Surely, I thought, this must be like the Paradise that Adam and Eve knew before they fell into the chaos of sin. How anguished they must have been to leave it. How they must have missed it, dreamed about it, and desperately yearned to go back to the Quiet. The thought left me as sad as a painting I once saw. A closed gate, a sworded angel, and two sets of footprints leading out of the Garden, out of the Quiet Place, out of Paradise. Away from the Father-Creator.

Surely, I thought, this is how Moses felt when he journeyed high upon the wilderness mountaintop—to the Quiet—and there spoke directly with God. He left the crowds of complaining people, people sorely unhappy with blistered feet and mediocre manna. Children asking him, "Moses, when will we get to the Promised Land?" and "Are we there yet?" Adults longing for left-behind Egyptian pleasures, having forgotten the pain of living as slaves to Egypt's elite. On that mountain, high above the crowds, a weary Moses found solitude and rest with his Father, the One who had created him to crave the Quiet.

But Moses had to climb down from Mt. Sinai. He had to once again face the glittery golden calves of a consumer-compelled society. I, too, had to descend Kappal and, once again, become part of the noisy human race. Had I not missed my husband and children so much, I could have stayed forever. With no distractions, prayer proved effortless, as natural as breathing. For hours at a time, I laid on my back on a blanket in the snow and gazed up into heaven. I watched the sun rise each morning with an explosion of midnight blue and rose and crème. I watched the sun set each evening with spectacular splashes of watercolor before blackness overcame the clouded skies. As I walked the paths, I saw, as if for the first time, the individual shapes of small rocks, the outline of trees against the sky, the smooth flight of streamlined birds. Without whizzing cars, blinking signs, red lights, green lights, the hypnotic glare of television tubes, meaningless radio music, and unending noise, I could concentrate solely on God's nature—sights and sounds I had failed to notice in my own noisy neon world.

My moments with God in solitude became sacred moments. I could hear His soft, sweet whispers, much like Elijah did in the Middle-Eastern mountains. High upon Mt. Horeb, Elijah learned something valuable about his relationship with Almighty God. He discovered that the Lord doesn't often speak in great and powerful winds, winds so fierce they tear mountains apart and shatter rocks. He discovered that the Lord doesn't often speak in the earthquake or in the fire. He can, but He doesn't. God spoke to Elijah in a "gentle whisper." Fortunately Elijah was listening. He listened even in the midst of natural chaos and confusion. So dramatically did God speak to him, Elijah covered his face with the hem of his cloak, in reverence and awe of the living Lord (see 1 Kings 19:9–13).

After three days I stepped off Kappal's mountain and back into life, into a culture of conflict and chaos and competition and caretaking. I came back to society's world, where people shun solitude, where people journey instead toward bright Las Vegas lights. But I came back with a freshly renewed mind. I had given my mind time to rest. My time at Kappal helped me better understand the meaning of solitude and quiet and rest and peace. It helped me rethink what is important in this life and what is not.

It has been seventeen years since I climbed down the mountain and left Kappal. I came home and immediately stepped back into a demanding life. During those years, I reared two high-energy toddlers to adulthood. I also worked tiring and difficult jobs both inside and outside my home. Some were high-powered and competitive. Others involved around-the-clock caretaking.

During the past seventeen years, I have dealt with the demands of marriage and family, of ministry and finances, of fragile relationships and fatigue, of ringing phones, sleepless nights, and inhumane deadlines. I have spent long nights tending feverish children, or worrying about young teenagers with new driver's licenses. I have walked long roads of cancer with sick friends. I have cried with a remaining spouse after her husband lost his battle with Alzheimer's. I have knelt at the bedside of my own dying father, prayed for his recovery, and grieved at his graveside.

Life has exhausted me. Each day has brought new demands, unexpected emergencies, and constant challenges. And just as Adam and Eve yearned to return to Paradise, I, too, have many times craved the uncomplicated quiet of Kappal.

I have not returned. I doubt I will ever again have that unique opportunity. But I have kept the quiet secrets of the Swiss mountain's monastery close to my heart. And sometimes, in my dreams, I go back to Kappal. Once again I commune with my Creator in the Quiet, and I stroke the heads of the contented cows on the Swiss mountainside.

FINDING QUIET TIME

How can you and I find quiet time, reflection time, prayer time, and mind-rest in a society of ever-increasing chaos and noise? How can we develop a deeper relationship with God within the clamor of our everyday hectic schedules? I am convinced that we must find a way to escape the confusion, the business and busy-ness of ordinary life, so that we can enter into the Quiet where God waits for us. But how do we do this? And why must we do this?

Once in a great while we can "escape" it, find a quiet Kappal, and allow our minds to rest in solitude. But for most of us, day-to-day routine rules out a trip to the Swiss mountaintops. Somehow we must find our Kappals within the midst of our everyday lives, whatever they hold. It is necessary that we spend time in solitude. And it is urgent that we find rest for our mind, body, and spirit. God has made us for rest. Jesus calls us to "Come to the Quiet Place . . . and find rest." He isn't talking about taking a two-week vacation from our workplace and splashing around in the ocean. He is telling us to make regular rest a high priority in our everyday lives, an everyday event. When we do, when we learn to seek the Quiet as Christ has commanded us to, we discover its secrets, and we hear God's whisper.

How nice it would be if every time we needed a quiet hour we could head to a twelfth-century monastery on a mountaintop in Switzerland! For most of us, myself included, time and duties and finances keep us closer to home. We can't manage an expensive retreat and days of quiet even when our minds scream for it. That's the wonderful advantage of coming to the Quiet, to the One who waits for us to come to Him within the chaos of an ordinary day. We don't have to *go* anywhere! We can come to the Quiet wherever we are, whenever we yearn for Him. Why? Because the Quiet is always within our reach. Because coming to the Quiet means coming to Jesus.

A JACKSON, TENNESSEE, WAFFLE HOUSE

I recently had an amazing experience in the Quiet with Christ. It happened in the most unlikely place: a busy, noisy waffle house!

My daughter, Alyce, had just begun her freshman year at Union University, and I drove the five-hour trip to Jackson to see her. We arranged to meet at 10:00 that morning at the local waffle house. I arrived at 9:30, found a bright orange booth, and ordered hot coffee. Alyce called at 10:00 to tell me she would be there at 10:30. So I sipped my coffee, and watched and waited for her.

As I sat there in that booth, I thought I had stepped into a circus. The jukebox jumped in the background. Two cooks shouted at each other and slung dark grease on the sizzling grill in front of me. Another cracked a handful of eggs and tossed them at the stove. Weary waitresses screamed orders to the grill cooks as they slapped down raw bacon and scraped up fried hash browns. "Peeeecan waffle! Bacon on the side! Dooooouble order hash browns! Two eggs—sunny-side-up!"

What a madhouse! A customer's cigarette smoke curled up around my cheeks. Mobs of hungry people rushed through the front door and scrambled to find a clean booth. Uncombed teenagers gobbled up sausage and eggs, then raced to their cars to reenter the highway. Kids cried loudly in the booths behind me while they waited for their breakfast. The ting-ting-ting of the cash register vibrated in my ear.

This place proved a miniature slice of life from the pages of the everyday world. My, my, my—for a quiet-loving person, I should have been pulling out my hair! But I wasn't. Instead, I experienced one of the most peaceful rests I've ever known.

As I watched the bacon grease fly and listened to the babies cry, I mentally stepped out of that noisy waffle house and into the Quiet Place. And in all the noise and smoke and chaos, Jesus met me there. He and I communed without words; we communicated mind to mind, heart to heart. Together we watched the harried and hurried people gulp down their grits, pick up their purses, pay their bills, and scurry away.

"Does he know you, Jesus?" I asked Him when a young man stood to pay his bill.

"That woman is hurting, isn't she, Lord?" I asked when a stranger's face clearly revealed her secret pain.

"Jesus, please put your loving arms around that lone elderly man over there. He looks like he needs Someone to love him."

For one whole hour Jesus and I talked, interrupted only when a waitress splashed a refill of coffee in the direction of my cup. By the time my daughter arrived, my mind had deeply rested.

I decided that morning that if I could find rest in that chaotic waffle house, I could find rest anywhere! I have started to come more often to the Quiet now, to that secret place where Jesus and I speak heart to heart. I find I can rest my mind in other challenging places, too, places where noisy activity seeks to overwhelm me—while stuck in afternoon traffic rushes, while standing in long grocery checkout lines, while listening to someone's meaningless chatter.

SHARING THE QUIET

I have also found that when I freshly emerge from the restful Quiet, I can share the Quiet with those around me. When a tired little girl threw a temper tantrum in the middle of the grocery-store pizza aisle, I surprised myself with my automatic response toward her.

I stopped my cart, and with her frazzled mother's permission, stooped to the floor, put my arms around her, and picked her up. Holding her in my arms, I smiled. The unexpected gesture of kindness immediately quieted her. Around my neck I wore a thin gold chain with a tiny mirror attached to it.

"Do you see that beautiful little girl in this mirror?" I asked her as I held the mirror up to her tear-smeared face. She caught her reflection and smiled. I slipped the necklace off my neck and onto hers. Then I gave her back to her mother. Her mother, who had stood watching this scene in utter amazement, thanked me and continued her shopping. I had been given the opportunity to share a moment of quiet and rest with an anxious little girl, and I thanked God for the experience.

Surely had I not experienced the Quiet Place myself, I couldn't have shared it with this small child. I discovered in that grocery-store aisle that we can only give to others what God has given first to us.

"COME TO ME"

"Come to Me," Jesus says in Matthew 11:28. "Come to me, all you who labor and are heavy laden, and I will give you rest" (NKJV).

I have discovered, both on a Swiss mountaintop and in a

bright orange booth at a waffle house, that Jesus keeps His promise of rest to us. Jesus loves you and me. He stays close to us, and He waits for us to step out of the chaos of life and into the Quiet with Him. No matter where we are, no matter how loud the noise, no matter how confusing the chaos, God is there. We can rest our anxious minds in Him. He is closer to us than our hands and feet, and nearer to us than our breathing. He is our Creator, and He created our minds to come to Him in the Quiet.

Chapter Three

MIND ATTACK!

If God created our minds to be bathed and refreshed by the Quiet, why have we, as a society, allowed our world to become such a noisy place? Why have we filled up every silent space around us with "clanging cymbals"? These days every car has a radio, every family room has a CD player, and almost every bedroom has a television set. Noise surrounds us—in our homes, in our cars, in our culture! Certainly it hasn't always been this way.

I chuckled not long ago when I heard about the sentencing of Edward Bello. Bello had committed some minor crime and expected to end up in jail. Instead, the judge sentenced him to nine months without television, saying he wanted "to create a condition of silent introspection" to help Bello change his behavior!

The judge ordered Bello to turn off the seven TV sets in his home, and Bello's outraged lawyers called the sentence "cruel and unusual punishment"—they considered jail time to be easier![1]

My grandparents remembered a quieter lifestyle. "Mama"

and "Papa" married in 1919, and by the time Charles Lindberg had made his famous thirty-three-hour transatlantic flight, they had birthed their third and final baby. They set up their home in a small farming community atop Sand Mountain, Alabama. They used a horse and wagon for rare trips into town. They walked to Sunday morning services at their church. They grew their own food, enough for their family and for the families who lived around them—they had food to eat and food to give away. Social life was family, community, and church. They met with neighbors and fellow church members, and together ate shared covered-dish dinners, what they called "dinner on the ground." In the evenings, they washed up the supper dishes, prepared the animals for the night, read the Bible and prayed as a family, and readied themselves for bed. When darkness fell upon their small farmhouse, they said good night and went to sleep. When the sun came up the next morning, they woke, ate a hearty breakfast, dressed for the day, and set about their work. They slipped their lives into the scheduled rhythm of nature, sunrise and sunset, and lived day by day with nature's rhythms of work and rest.

My grandparents worked hard. They shared their food and their faith. They enjoyed their family and friends. They worshiped God both personally and within a congregation. They knew quiet days. They had long hours to pray while they planted and harvested their vegetable gardens, and while they canned corn and tomatoes for the lengthy winter months. They had the early evening hours of darkness to lie in bed and meditate. They allowed their minds to wonder and dream and ask questions about life and love and God.

Of course they had their worries and concerns during their long lives. After all, they went through a devastating Depression, two world wars, personal sickness and surgery, the deaths of parents and brothers and sisters, the problems of parenthood and grandparenthood. Yet even during their hardest days, they kept a quiet mind, a mind immersed in the quiet rituals of each day, a mind centered on Christ's constant presence.

In 1925, the year my mother was born to them, Papa bought a Victrola. Three large thick records came with it. They wound it up once in a while and listened together. Papa gave me the old Victrola a few years before he died. It was like brand-new. It had a perfect wooden case, the original steel needle made in Paris, and the three old records, unscratched.

My grandparents treasured their quiet hours. They allowed nothing, not even a newly invented Victrola, to interrupt those God-given quiet times when they thought and prayed and pondered and rested their minds. Some years after the Depression, Papa bought his family a radio. They listened to the president declare war, and they used the radio to keep up with war news.

Years later they bought a black-and-white television set. For half an hour at noon, and another at night, they learned what was happening in the world. Then the television set was shut off, and they gathered to pray for family, friends, and those hurting people spotlighted on that day's news broadcasts.

The daily habits they set in 1919, when they first established their home together, followed them throughout their lengthened lives. I remember much from my childhood about my beloved grandparents and their small, white gabled farmhouse. I remember family socials and wonderful holiday meals and aunts and uncles and cousins. I remember long walks with Mama through her flower gardens. I remember feeding watermelon rinds to the backyard pony, Inky, and playing with the assortment of grandkids, gentle old dogs, chickens, and one hard-boiled turkey. I remember hot summer afternoons as I sat in the kitchen and listened to the rain that interrupted my outside play.

But most of all, I remember the tranquility and the quiet. The only background noises were nature's sounds—the abrupt bark of "Little Man," the hickory nuts falling from the trees, and the wind rustling autumn leaves.

Even now I often lie in bed and dream about that little farmhouse located somewhere between heaven and Paradise. I retrace my steps among the backyard trees and sing the songs about Jesus my grandfather taught me. I sit on the back porch with its tin roof, and I pop green beans, fresh from the garden, with my grandmother. And I ponder our silence together, a silence broken only by the snap and tap of broken beans as they drop into the red-rimmed, white enamel bowl.

My grandparents taught me to love the Quiet. For half a century, I have tried desperately to hold on to that treasured gift, a gift from the past that few children or adults today remember or cherish. The Quiet—the place for which our minds were made; the place in which our minds are mentored; the place in which our minds are re-created. God made our minds for the Quiet, and patiently He waits for us there, whispering softly, "Come . . . Come to the Quiet."

THE DEATH OF SILENCE

Had the death of silence come suddenly, we might have noticed it. Had the terrible enemy, Noise, ascended on us one night, wreaked its havoc, and killed the Quiet, maybe we would have gathered up arms and fought it.

H. G. Wells' quiet English villagers of 1898 knew about terrible enemies that descended suddenly on them one day; they tried to fight the sudden invasion of Martians in Wells' *The War of the Worlds*. They had not nearly the strength and technology of those "vast spiderlike machines, nearly a hundred feet high, capable of the speed of an express train, and able to shoot out a beam of intense heat."[2]

Wells wrote,

> No one would have believed in the last years of the nineteenth century that this world was being watched keenly and closely by intelligences greater than man's. . . . As men busied themselves about their various concerns

they were scrutinised and studied. . . . Intellects vast and cool and unsympathetic, regarded this earth with envious eyes, and slowly and surely drew their plans against us.[3]

The invasion comes quickly, while the people of England go about their ordinary affairs. With no warning,

The air [is] full of sound, a deafening and confusing conflict of noises—the clangorous din of the Martians, the crash of falling houses, the thud of trees, fences, sheds flashing into flames, and the crackling and roaring of fire.[4]

People flee from their homes, crowd into the streets, and run for their lives.

People were fighting savagely for standing-room in the carriages . . . people were being trampled and crushed . . . revolvers were fired, people stabbed, and the policemen who had been sent to direct the traffic, exhausted and infuriated, were breaking the heads of the people they were called out to protect.[5]

In one night the valley had become a valley of ashes. . . . Where flames had been there were now streamers of smoke. . . . The countless ruins of shattered and gutted houses and blasted and blackened trees . . . stood out now gaunt and terrible.[6]

Wells describes vividly the results of the unexpected invasion, the "sad, haggard women tramping by, well dressed, with children that cried and stumbled, their dainty clothes smothered in dirt, their weary faces smeared with tears."[7]

The Martians disrupted the villagers and killed the Quiet quickly. The people immediately recognized the deadly enemy that descended suddenly on them from Mars. They fought the Martians with all their strength and power. They knew they could not possibly live with the "sharp, resinous tang of burning . . . in the air."[8]

Nevertheless, I wonder how H. G. Wells' village people would have reacted had the enemy not struck swiftly, but rather had come slowly into their midst? What if the Martians had come camouflaged, learned Earth-people's ways, and lived purposely among them for a while? What if the enemy had offered entertainment, laughter, thrills, and companionship to Earth's citizens?

Would the people have even noticed the "huge black shapes, grotesque and strange, [that moved] busily to and fro"? Would the children have "cried and stumbled . . . their weary faces smeared with tears"? Would the people have fled from their homes, crowded into the streets, and run for their very lives?

Probably not. They might not have even noticed the entrance of the enemy. Unafraid, perhaps they would have grown accustomed to the hardly detected aliens. They might have even opened the front doors of their homes to them, invited them into their family rooms, placed them by the hearth, and opened their hearts and eyes and ears to absorb the deadly messages.

Is this not what the enemy Noise has done to our society? It has slowly descended into our midst and captured our interest. We have allowed the enemy to live close to our hearths and hearts, to entertain us, to provide us with companionship. He follows us everywhere we go. We have become accustomed to his constant presence. We have welcomed him. We have given him our vulnerable minds—minds created to think and ponder; minds created for the Quiet. With each new year and each new generation, we allow the enemy a stronger foothold.

> The truth is that the dangers to which we are most vulnerable are generally not the sudden, dramatic, obvious ones. They are the ones that creep up on us, that are so much a part of our environment that we don't even notice them.[9]

The enemy Noise has crept up on us. Few of us notice him

living in our midst. He is working his devastation even now, bombarding our minds minute by minute, hour by hour, day by day, year after year. He has squeezed out the very life of Quiet, strangling him with mind-torturing heavy-metal instruments and annoying background music. He has seized our minds and saturated them with deliberate sound pollution. Our Quiet-loving minds cry out for relief from the confusion, but those wails are drowned out by Noise. Unless we consciously flee to a lonely place, we must contend with society's ever-present alien: Noise.

We have grown so used to the familiar stranger in our home, many of us can no longer live without him. Take our television away from us for nine months, and we, like Edward Bello, cry out, "Cruel and unusual punishment!"

We face Noise wherever we go. Noise, disguised as background music, follows us from the grocery store to the department store. We meet with friends at a favorite restaurant, and intimate talk is overwhelmed by the nuisance Noise. Bookstores, coffee shops, elevators, and even telephone waiting lines are wired to produce the drone of meaningless music. Is there no escape from the tumult that assaults our ears? What about in our own private homes? Are we spared from Noise there? Hardly!

I encourage you to listen to the sounds in your home on any given day. In most American homes today, the alien has set up house there and infiltrates and influences every moment. He slithers through radios, stereos, televisions, telephones, personal computers, CD players, DVD devices, electronic games, kitchen gadgets, coffee-bean grinders, battery-operated toothbrushes, blow-dryers, and the vast assembly of miscellaneous home appliances that clang, beep, and hum in the backgrounds of our lives. We have become so accustomed to the enemy, we seldom read a book or eat a meal without his presence. He's always there with us, concertedly keeping our minds from resting in the Quiet.

Not only are we deluged with earfuls of constant noise but our eyes have also become open ears. Just when we learn to filter out some of the noise that bombards our ears, the enemy starts to influence us with "eye noise." Except to close our eyelids, we cannot escape it. It shouts to us from billboards as we drive down the highways. It blinks to us in neon lights when we enter a department store or restaurant. It flashes to us beneath church steeples calling us to loud church "worship" services. It announces sales, warnings, statistics, and sayings on every street corner. It seems that everyone with anything to say or sell fights for the consumers' eye attention. We see inscribed messages on teenagers' T-shirts, on car bumpers, and on babies' bibs! Everyone has a statement, a philosophy that he wants desperately to share. We have become a society bombarded with images and messages, pictures and projects that shout for our attention, neon signs that financially compete with each other to call us out of the Quiet and into the chaos.

ESCAPE FROM CHAOTIC CONTEMPORARY LIFE

I hear more and more of families who yearn to return to my grandparents' simple, soundproofed way of life. Not long ago I read the fascinating story of Scott Savage and his family. Scott, along with his wife, Mary Ann, and their young children decided to leave the fast-paced American lifestyle. They made a new home with a Quaker community in Barnesville, Ohio. They gave up their car, electricity, television, radio, and all other modern conveniences. They either walk or commute around town, sometimes riding Ned, a temperamental old horse. Scott and Mary Ann have given up driver's licenses, social security cards, travel, and the hospital births of their children.

Scott finds a special joy in walking instead of driving. He learns about "the songbirds and the ditches, the bridges and the particular silhouettes of the distant hills, quietly, intimately, as only the walkers of the world experience." He has discovered that walking "leaves me feeling I have exited time to participate in the eternal 'now' of creation. It puts me in a relationship of reverie and praise for all I see."[10]

The Savages usually worship with the Quiet-loving Quaker community. He writes,

> Silence! What a remarkable thing that it still exists at the end of the twentieth century, here in our little meetinghouse. Moreover, these people are gathered together in the silence for a purpose: to wait upon the Lord.[11]

At other times the Savages plan quiet worship services in their home.

> There is deep satisfaction to be found in sitting quietly for an hour with a calm and silent child leaning back against you. . . . The ministry that occurs is usually in the form of singing soft hymns on which we all often join in. But most of the time is spent in a richer quiet than may ever be experienced by many people today. It . . . is a blessed replacement for the . . . life of career, commute, consume that Mary Ann and I have given up.[12]

On one occasion, the Savages took their children on a train ride to learn about their local history. By this time they had become pleasingly settled into the silent, unhurried Quaker lifestyle. As they stood in a long line to board the train,

> Mary Ann and I exchanged looks. An intense feeling of alienation began to grow in my gut as I stood there in a crowd of my fellow Americans. It's a curious thing, this sensation that I've experienced in public places all of my adult life. And it had only grown stronger in that year spent among the very, very modestly dressed and physically fit Amish of Holmes County.[13]

While standing in a line of loud, noisy people from outside the Quaker community, Scott reflects: "The differences in behavior and appearance encountered in the larger world have come to seem ever more amazing and bizarre."[14]

Somehow we Quiet-yearning Christians must carve out space in the lonely places where we might retreat to rest with Quiet. We must escape the air "full of sound, a deafening and confusing conflict of noises." We must run and hide from the "clangorous din of the Martians."

But how? How can you and I find a quiet mind in a society held hostage by the enemy Noise? That will be the focus of our next two chapters.

Chapter Four

RESTING OUR MIND IN CHRIST

We can come to the Quiet! We can obey Jesus' command. "Come to Me," He offers. "Come to the Quiet." But how can you and I do this in the midst of an increasingly busy society?

Charles Swindoll informs us,

> It doesn't require a Ph.D. from Princeton to assess that we are busy, busy, busy. Forever on the move, doing things, eating stuff, working, jumping, jogging, writing, marrying, divorcing, buying . . . you name it, our country is doing it. . . . The pace is somewhere between maddening and insane. The freeways are shocked with traffic, people are going or coming twenty-four hours every day . . . with no letup in sight. Faces reflect tension. The air is polluted. The earth shakes. The malls are crowded. Nerves are shot.[1]

How can you and I find the Quiet Place—the place of worship, reverence, and awe—escaping the place located "somewhere between maddening and insane"—when our minds have been conditioned by artificial techno-noise, when "our brains are no longer conditioned for reverence and awe?"[2]

Over the past fifty years or so, television and the media, not creative and worshipful silence, have molded our minds, zapped our attention spans, and glazed over our eyes.

> First radio, then television, have assaulted and over-turned the privacy of the home, the real American privacy, which permitted the development of a higher and more independent life within democratic society. Parents can no longer control the atmosphere of the home and have lost even the will to do so.[3]

How can we celebrate solitude when our weary minds are constantly surrounded and assaulted by chaos?

It's time to get practical here. Let me share with you a few mind-resting suggestions that have worked for me and for others, and that might work for you too.

- *Television*. Turn off your television set. I've been in some homes where the TV stays on all day and all evening. TV has become like an adopted member of the family! Television can become a noisy, time-eating habit. Plan the programs you want to watch. Before the programs begin, and after the programs end, keep the television turned off. You don't need the constant background chatter. Larry Burkett writes about the effects of television on the minds of today's children:

  > The net result is a nearly brain-dead generation of kids growing up on the garbage dished out by the most liberal segment of our society: the media. There are some good things on TV, but you have to pick and choose carefully for your kids and for yourself as well.[4]

- *Special Places*. Find a special place in your home or garden or office where you can escape for a few minutes of solitude during the day. It may be a favorite chair in your bedroom.

Or a bench in your garden. Or a couch in the ladies' room at your office building. Any place will do, as long as you can enjoy a moment of Quiet alone. When you visit your place of Quiet, sit in silence for a few minutes. In doing so, you will be taking a break from the noise pollution that constantly surrounds you. Visit your Quiet Place as often as you can. These moments will refresh your mind.

- *Tune Out Noise.* When you cannot "escape" to a place of Quiet, learn how to tune out the noise around you.

  (1) Think about the most lovely place you've ever been.
  (2) Lose yourself by looking at a restful painting of a nature scene.
  (3) Relax your body.
  (4) Breathe deeply.
  (5) Concentrate mentally on the One who loves you, the One who gave himself for you. Be aware of Him, for He stands beside you.
  (6) Surround your workplace with meaningful and beautiful things such as flowers and pictures and pottery.

  In doing so, you will be resisting the work of the enemy Noise. Did you know that recent studies on "noise pollution" state that noise can cause certain health problems, such as cardiovascular disease, impaired speech ability, increased blood pressure and stress hormone levels, sleep disturbance, etc.? Ordinary environmental noise can cause a variety of symptoms, including anxiety, emotional stress, nervous complaints, nausea, headaches, instability, argumentativeness, sexual impotency, changes in mood, increase in social conflicts, and general psychiatric disorders such as neurosis, psychosis, and hysteria. High levels of environmental noise can cause deteriorated mental health. Noise can have the most damaging effect on the elderly, ill, or depressed; people with particular diseases or medical problems; people dealing with complex cognitive tasks; the blind and hearing-impaired; fetuses, babies, and young children. High-level, continuous noise can contribute to "feelings of helplessness" among school children.[5]

Resist Distractions. Catherine Marshall advises,

> Shut out distractions—the doorbell, the telephone, the [delivery person], the children['s playing]. . . . God asks that we worship Him with concentrated minds. . . . A divided and scattered mind is not at its most receptive.[5]

- *Make This Your Daily Prayer:*

> Lord God, there is so much noise in my world, in my life, that makes it difficult to hear my own inner thoughts, let alone listen to the Words of Your beloved Son. Help me to acquire the kind of inner peace that will open my being to Your Word so that I can respond appropriately.[6]

- *Recite Scripture.* During stressful times, close your eyes and recite from memory a favorite Bible verse. Strive to memorize those verses that will bring rest to your overworked mind.
- *Pray Constantly.* It takes only seconds to tell the Lord that you love Him. Pray sentence prayers throughout your busy days. Constant prayer will keep your mind constantly on Christ.
- *Vacate.* Plan mental vacations. Choose a morning or afternoon, and plan to sit and ponder alone quietly. Use this time of solitude to think about your life and its priorities. Think about your faith. Count your blessings. Pray aloud without interruptions. A morning and/or afternoon spent in the Quiet with Jesus will fill you deeply with His refreshing Living Water.

- *Trade Kids.* If you have small children, and if you have a good friend with small children, take turns caring for all the children, and each enjoy a few hours of Quiet on your afternoons alone.
- *Go to the Library.* Visit your local community library as often as you can. It's usually quiet there. In fact, the library remains one of the few places society gives us that offers rest from noise. Give yourself time to browse through the rows of books. Sit. Read. Lose yourself in classic and contemporary works. Join the thoughts and experiences of authors of yesterday and today. Check out books. Plan quiet times during your busy days at home to read.
- *Spend Time at a Church.* If possible, walk to a nearby church during your busy days. Find a comfortable pew. Spend a few moments in the Quiet and pray.
- *Read Children's Books.* Visit the children's section of your local library. Sit in the Quiet with a lapful of beautifully illustrated books. Children's volumes employ the best authors and artists. They celebrate shape and color. Enjoy the pictures. Read the ones you loved as a child.
- *Make a List.* Find pencil and paper and keep them close to you. Write down those things you must do. Give your mind a rest from trying to remember all the things you must accomplish throughout the day.
- *Don't Sweat!* "Don't sweat the small stuff." Decide what things are important enough to think about. Do only those things that are necessary. Give your brain a rest from responsibility.
- *Solicit Help.* Let people assist you with necessary projects, such as baby showers, office tasks, and evening dinners. When someone offers to help you, take her up on it!
- *Use Earplugs.* Buy a good pair of earplugs. And wear them!
- *Unplug and Turn Off.* Check the noise levels in your home. Decide what you can unplug or turn off to lower the noise

volume. Listen for all those noises you've grown accustomed to hearing. If possible, get rid of them.

- *Expect Consideration.* Ask family members to be quieter at home. Teach children to speak more softly indoors. Keep television, radio, computers, and other noisy devices at a lower volume. Practice being quieter as a family.
- *Have Quiet Mealtimes.* Decrease the chaos at family mealtimes. Ask each family member to sit quietly at the dinner table. On some evenings, plan "silent" meals together while you eat. Teach your children the benefits of silence.
- *Rise Earlier.* Get up earlier on some mornings. Enjoy the Quiet and solitude. Sit in the dark with your eyes closed. Listen to your breathing. Take this time to thank God for your mind and for your God-given ability to think and ponder and pray. Thank Him for your wonderfully created body. Thank Him for family and friends. Thank Him for His gift of grace. Praise Him with thanksgiving for all His many gifts of blessing to you and your family.
- *Celebrate Friendship.* Plan a special evening for a quiet dinner with a friend that you trust. Choose a restaurant where noise is minimal. Or take a picnic dinner to a quiet park setting. Converse from your heart with your friend. Tell her your problems, your frustrations. Share with her your ambitions, your goals. Dream together. Encourage each other. Pray together. Remember that we women are relational creatures. We need a loving, listening ear. And we need to lend our own loving, listening ears to those women who also need to talk. Cherish your friendships with women who are trustworthy, those who love the Lord and who also love you.
- *Reflect.* Take time to remember and reflect on your life. I often take a mental vacation in the middle of a busy workday by remembering fun times during my childhood, or special times with family and friends. Pull out old photo albums.

Relive those special times spent with people you have loved and trusted.

- *Make Quiet Time.* Go to bed earlier at night. Take the moments before you drift off to sleep to pray and think and ponder. Use this quiet time to pray, read Scripture, and meditate.
- *Home Telephones.* Take the telephone off the hook when you want to enjoy some uninterrupted Quiet time at home.
- *Silence Your Cell Phone.* Turn off your cell phone. When you shop or work or eat, leave your cell phone in the car. Keep your cell phone for emergencies rather than for calling convenience.
- *Stop Worrying.* Worry can become a habit. Give your worries to the Lord. Ask Him to settle your mind about them. Memorize this Scripture verse:

  Do not be anxious about anything, but in everything, by prayer and petition, with thanksgiving, present your requests to God. [Then enjoy] the peace of God, which transcends all understanding, [which] will guard your hearts and *your minds* in Christ Jesus. (Philippians 4:6–7, emphasis mine)

- *Respect and Reserve Space.* Teach your children to respect another person's quiet and space. Encourage your kids to spend some time on their own playing or reading quietly. Be careful not to over-schedule your children's daily activities.
- *Preexamine Noise Levels.* Before you purchase an item, consider the amount of noise it will make. This is especially true when you consider buying an electronic item. Beware of devices that will hum, beep, or clatter, disturbing your family's quiet times together.
- *Rest Your Brain.* In order to operate at peak performance and to learn/remember new skills, our brain needs its rest! Dr. Sara C. Mednick, a Harvard psychologist, writes about a new

study on minds and rest and learning: "The brain needs sleep to incorporate newly learned skills into the permanent memory."[8] Take naps! Find time to rest and re-create your mind!

- *Ponder.* Take the apostle Paul's advice:

> Whatever is true, whatever is noble, whatever is right, whatever is pure, whatever is lovely, whatever is admirable—if anything is excellent or praiseworthy—think about these things. (Philippians 4:8)

No doubt you have many ideas of your own about how to bring delightful peace and quiet into daily chaos and how to eliminate unnecessary noise from your office and home. These are but a few suggestions. Remember that God created our minds for Quiet. Our minds need regular rest from worries, stress, and the pressures of noise and daily life.

Heed the call of Jesus when He calls you to "come . . . Come to the Quiet." He has much to say to you and me. He has much to teach us in the Quiet Place. He wants to fill our minds with His refreshing Living Water. He wants to enrich our minds with His wisdom, His words, and His encouragement. Come to the Quiet. He waits for you there. Listen to Him speak to you. After a few minutes with Him in the Quiet Place, you'll step back into the bustling world with a changed mind, a mind that Christ himself will begin to transform.

Chapter Five

LETTING CHRIST TRANSFORM OUR MIND

If God were to make a human brain, what kind of perfection would scientists marvel at?"[1]

The brain is an incredible organ:

> A whole person lies inside the bony box, locked in, protected, sealed away from the indispensable duties of managing one hundred trillion cells in a human body. The Head of the Body is the seat of mystery and wisdom and unity.[2]

Nobel laureate Roger Sperry exclaims that within the brain are

> imagination, morality, sensuality, mathematics, memory, humor, judgment, religion . . . an incredible catalog of facts and theories and common sense. There are forces within forces within forces, as in no other cubic half-foot of the universe that we know.[3]

Surely there is nothing on earth so wonderful as the human

mind that God created and set within our "bony box"! "The three-pound human brain, five hundred million times more complicated than our most advanced computer, is being called 'the new frontier.' "[4]

Who can fathom its intricate, complex design? Eric Chaisson, who received his doctorate in astrophysics from Harvard University, has described the human brain as "the most exquisitely complex clump of matter in the known universe."[5]

Can you believe that today's scientists think they can duplicate the brain? It's true! Day after day, since 1984, teams of programmers, linguists, theologians, mathematicians, and philosophers have plugged away at a $60-million project to teach a computer, named "Cye," to think and use common sense. Scientists hope to create Cye into a "self-organizing system that would then learn on its own."

Good luck! Surely, only God can create such a remarkable thinking "machine" as the human mind.[6]

Missionary doctor Paul Brand writes,

> The whole mental process comes down to these ten billion cells spitting irritating chemicals at each other across the synapses or gaps. The brain's total number of connections rivals the stars and galaxies of the universe.[7]

You and I keep the neurons or nerve cells of our minds throughout our whole lives. *All our other cells age and are replaced about every seven years.* Your skin, eyes, heart, and bones are entirely different today from those you carried around just one decade ago. But what makes you YOU—your brain—stays the same, "maintaining the continuity of selfhood that keeps the entity of [YOU] alive."[8]

Your mind is an amazing miracle! Scripture tells us, "Let this *mind* be in you which was also in Christ Jesus" (Philippians 2:5 KJV, emphasis mine). In other words, Paul tells us to become "Christ-minded"; we are to follow Christ into the Quiet with our minds. Several things happen to our minds when we do this.

As you and I spend time with Christ, we become more like Him. As our mind rests in Christ, we regain our sense of awe and reverence, of worship and wonder. Becoming Christ-minded means that we begin to think like Jesus Christ himself. We think His thoughts. He fills our minds with His words. He teaches us to discern more clearly His gentle whisper. We learn to recognize His voice when He speaks our name and calls us to the Quiet Place to be with Him.

"Once we have committed ourselves to spending time in solitude, we develop an attentiveness to God's voice in us."[9]

The more time we spend with Christ in the Quiet, the more in tune with Him our minds become. We hear Him! We develop a deeper awareness of God's presence weaving throughout the ordinary hours of our lives. We begin to see the world around us through His eyes. Our worldview conforms to His worldview. We see other people as Jesus sees them. We peer beneath the "masks" people wear. We look deep into their hearts and minds and learn their pains and concerns. We learn to "read between the lines" of a person's life and speech. Christ enables us to better reach out to help those around us who are hurting. We experience compassion; we learn to empathize, to identify with, and to suffer with the wounded of this world.

As we spend time with Christ in the Quiet Place, we learn to better appreciate the Quiet. We come to crave the Quiet as an animal craves water on a hot, dry day. *The more time we spend in the Quiet, the more time we will want to spend there.*

When we reduce the volume of noise around us, we will begin to hear sounds we haven't heard before. Softer sounds will delight us. Sounds like the heartfelt question a small child asks. Or the peeping of newly hatched birds in a nest. Or crickets chirping at night under our bedroom window. Or soft winds blowing through tree branches on a gentle day. Or the sound a stream makes as it flows over smooth rocks. When we immerse ourselves in the Quiet, we will learn how to truly listen.

The Quiet creates within our minds a keener sense of concentration when we give ourselves time to contemplate. Gone will be surface thoughts. Our thoughts will run much deeper, and our conversations will become more meaningful. We will take nothing at face value anymore. We will ponder the deeper meanings of another's unexpected action or careless word. What might have once upset us will no longer hold such irritating power over us. We will become more like Jesus in our actions. We will move through life as He did, with keener concentration, deeper concern for others; mind and motions will be unhurried, unfettered, no longer anxious.

Transformation begins in the mind. Transformation begins in the Quiet, when we set aside serious time to listen to the voice of God. Surely "we do not take the spiritual life seriously if we do not set aside some time to be with God and listen to Him!"[10]

Paul tells us about mind transformation when he writes, "Do not conform any longer to the pattern of this world, but *be transformed by the renewing of your mind*" (Romans 12:2, emphasis mine).

Mind transformation begins in the Quiet. What is the Quiet? It is Christ. The Quiet is the place of solitude where we can come to Christ, rest our minds, and request mental transformation.

"Without solitude it is virtually impossible to live a spiritual life. Solitude begins with a time and place for God, and Him alone."[11]

Paul urges, "*Let this mind be in you, which was also in Christ Jesus,* who, being in the form of God . . . took upon Him the form of a servant and was made in the likeness of men" (Philippians 2:5–7 KJV, emphasis mine).

Where is the Quiet? It's anywhere you want it to be.

It's a black Chevrolet and a grandmother's shoulder; it's a lonely monastery on a Swiss mountaintop; it's Jackson,

Tennessee's waffle-eating people with tired, weary faces; it's the clangorous din of Martians, once and for all time silenced; it's a prayerful Quaker meetinghouse and a temperamental old horse named Ned.

The Quiet is a mind set on Christ, and Christ alone. Surely those who live in accordance with the Spirit have their *minds* set on what the Spirit desires (Romans 8:5). "You will keep in perfect peace him whose *mind* is steadfast, because he trusts in you," writes Isaiah (26:3). "The *mind* controlled by the Spirit is life and peace" (Romans 8:6, all emphasis mine).

"Come to me," Jesus invites. "Come to me, all you who are weary and burdened, and I will give you rest" (Matthew 11:28).

What wonderful promises!

Section Two

BODY REST

JESUS SAID:
"COME TO ME, ALL YOU WHO LABOR . . ."
(MATTHEW 11:28 NKJV)

Chapter Six

TODAY'S WOMAN–OVERWORKED!

If you love your job, have plenty of quality time with your husband, kids, and friends, are satisfied with your time for homekeeping duties, and enjoy ample personal, quiet, devotional time with God, then you can skip this chapter—you don't need it! In fact, you should be writing this book! You are Superwoman, a rare and endangered species.

However, if you are one of the millions of women in this country who work too hard, are physically exhausted and stressed-out, have little quality time with her husband, kids, or friends, stay far behind in her housework, and have little or no quiet time for solitude and prayer, then keep reading. I wrote this chapter—and this book—just for you.

Perhaps you can identify with my friend Janice. Janice had tears streaming down her face when she confessed to me: "Denise, I feel like I'm on a treadmill. I work as hard as I can, and I still can't get everything done. I'm missing important deadlines at the office, my house is a mess, and my husband and kids are getting the worst leftover part of me at night. I come home from work each afternoon exhausted. I give what little energy I have left to my family. After I put the kids to bed at night, I have nothing left for my husband. I can tell you this: I can't keep this schedule much longer. It's just not working anymore! It's robbing all the joy from my life. What can I do?"

Janice stopped talking and looked at me as if she expected me to voice the perfect solution to her problem. I like Janice; we have been good friends for years. At the time, she had a high-profile job in a downtown law firm, a wonderful Christian husband, and three darling school-aged daughters.

In my heart, I wanted to ask her some brutally hard questions, questions I had struggled to answer just a few years earlier. But I bit my tongue. I didn't want to overstep the boundaries of our friendship. I told her this was a personal situation about which she must pray, think deeply, and make some definite decisions.

I simply told her, "No one but God can guide you and your family in making these choices. Only He knows what you and your family need." Even so, I assured Janice that I would pray for her as she sought the Lord's advice. I also suggested that she talk with a Christian counselor, a person who could look at her situation objectively, and then honestly discuss it with her.

"Look at the big picture of your life," I urged. "Pray diligently for God's guidance. Consider the needs of your family as well as your own physical and spiritual needs."

What were the "heart questions" I *yearned* to ask her—those painfully direct questions about her life, her work, her faith, her family, and her priorities? Those questions that God had directly pointed out to me? Here are some of them:

- "Exactly why are you working outside the home, Janice, when you could simplify your lifestyle and live without the extra income?"
- "Are you really physically able to continue this chaotic sched-

ule, and, if so, are you somehow harming your future health? Is the extra income you make worth the physical risks to your health?"

- "Have you somehow confused your work with your self-worth? Does your self-esteem come from your position, paycheck, and impressive credentials?"

- "Are you willing to possibly sacrifice your marriage and children for your work goals? Is full-time employment strangling your family time, and, if so, is the trade-off worth it?"

- "What are you teaching your daughters about life and faith priorities? Do you want them to follow in your hassled, hurried footsteps? What kind of example are you setting for them?"

If I had asked her these questions, I can only imagine what her answers would be. Janice had bought into the myth that women can do everything, and do everything perfectly: work a demanding full-time job, keep a beautiful, clean home, birth and rear children, keep a busy husband satisfied, grow her own herbs and vegetables, and play a great game of competitive tennis! Janice has been a woman swept along with the current American tide of "having it all, doing it all." She graduated from college and then graduate school, found a good job, married, had children, and never questioned her choice to work outside her home. Now after a few years of demanding responsibilities, she fights exhaustion, frustration with her own physical limitations, spiritual dryness, and loss of joy.

To stay abreast of current legal information, Janice found herself working harder and longer hours both at the office and at home. Her work hours gobbled up almost her entire family and personal time. Janice was completely wrapped up in her job; in fact, she had become her work. Her prestigious position became the fragile vessel that held her self-esteem. She believed her position gave her worth as a woman. In the meantime, Janice lived on the "treadmill," always running, always in a hurry, always too busy to kick off her shoes and rest. I knew it was just a matter of time before Janice wore out. And so did she.

OUR IMAGINARY CONVERSATION

As I drove home, I had an imaginary dialogue with Janice. One by one, I asked her the questions that lay so heavy on my heart. I could almost predict her answers.

DENISE: "Exactly why are you working outside the home, Janice, when you don't necessarily need the extra income?"

JANICE: "That's just what I do! I've never considered *not* working. Anyway, there's nothing wrong with working outside the home. I'm good at what I do. I like to have extra money to buy the luxuries I want. I can give my kids so much more than I had as a kid. And anyway, I spent too many years in graduate school learning this profession to quit my job and waste my talents."

DENISE: "Is the extra money worth your health? Are you really physically able to continue this chaotic schedule, and, if so, are you somehow harming your future health?"

JANICE: "I have to admit, Denise, that this schedule is killing me! The constant exhaustion is beginning to be a real problem now. I don't know how long I can keep this pace, but the alternative is to quit my job. I guess I could live without the extra money. But I don't want to quit! It's who I am, what I do. I don't know any other lifestyle."

DENISE: "Janice, have you somehow confused your work with your worth as a woman? Does your self-esteem come from your position, paycheck, and impressive credentials?"

JANICE: "Now, Denise, that's a personal question. I'd like to think about that one for a while. But I guess I am possibly too proud of my position, the size of my paycheck, and, yes, my credentials are impressive. But they are impressive because I have worked extremely hard in a competitive field. They have not come easily! But surely I don't consider my self-worth to come from my job . . . uh . . . do I?"

DENISE: "Janice, are you willing to possibly sacrifice your marriage and children to your work goals?"

JANICE: "Come on, Denise! I don't think I'm sacrificing my husband and children because I work an outside job! That sounds like an insult. I wouldn't purposely hurt my family. But I do feel that I just don't have enough time with them. We rush through supper, hurry through homework, and we don't have much evening time to talk and play together. To tell you the truth, I miss having downtime with them. They're growing up so quickly, and I'm not with them as much as I'd like to be. As for my husband, he works hard too. That's the American way, isn't it? We both want to do well. Yet I guess I have to admit that I miss him too. We try to have family devotions at supper—you know, Bible reading and prayer—but with homework, extra office work, soccer practice, and piano lessons—sometimes we just can't squeeze it in."

DENISE: "What are you teaching your daughters about life and faith priorities? Do you want them to follow in your hassled, hurried footsteps? What kind of example are you setting for them?"

JANICE: "That cuts to the bone, Denise! My answer is NO, NO, NO!! I certainly don't want my daughters to work all the time, always be behind in their schedules, never have time for themselves or their families, and lose the very joy of living. I don't want my grandchildren to have mothers who don't have time for them because of some demanding full-time job. But here again, I want my girls to be successful, have high self-esteem, and have a purpose for their lives."

I pray that one day Janice will figure it out, that she will learn to listen to her exhausted physical body, that she will give herself needed time to rest, and that she will set her priorities in order.

Maybe . . . with God's help . . . she will look at the big picture of her life, ask herself some tough personal questions, and then make life-changing choices that will enrich her own life as well as that of her family.

I also yearn to remind Janice that life is short. I have lost too many friends to death, friends that learned too late just how temporary human life can be. "The future is now," I wanted to tell her. "You may not have a tomorrow."

Listen to the psalmist: "Remember how fleeting is my life" (Psalm 89:47). Heed Scripture and pray with the psalmist: "Teach us to number our days aright, that we may gain a heart of wisdom" (Psalm 90:12).

WHAT I LONG TO YELL FROM THE ROOFTOPS!

Perhaps you are like Janice. I certainly used to be! You work too hard. You run yourself ragged. Your body is always exhausted. Too much to do, too busy to rest, never any time for yourself, little time and energy for your family, no daydream time, no lunches with friends, no fishing for bass from a quiet riverbank.

Have you ever stopped to ask yourself *why* you feel you must do everything you do? Yes, we all have work to do. Work is good. Work is rewarding. Work is necessary. But are you spreading yourself so thin that you are doing nothing as well as you would like to? Have you lost your joy of living? Are you "all work" and "no play"? Are you living in a rut, in the bottom of a deep, dull pit?

Whenever I meet a person like Janice, whenever I hear her inward heart's cry and her outward verbal frustration, I silently pray for her. Then I ask her to stop, put her hand on her heart, and quietly listen.

I'd like to say the same thing to you right now. Stop reading, take a deep breath, and place your hand over your heart. Quietly listen. Your heart knows a secret that most American women have never learned. God created your heart to beat and then to rest. Beat and rest. Beat and rest. Imagine what would happen to your heart, to your entire body, if your heart beat (worked) constantly and never stopped to rest! It would wear out in a very short time. Your heart works and rests in perfect harmony. It gives equal time to both work and rest. I believe this is the way God created your body—to work and rest, work and rest, in equal parts, in perfect harmony. Your heart knows what makes life balanced, an equal portion of work and rest. Will you stop and listen to the message of your heart?

Karl Rahner speaks for many exhausted women in this nation when he laments:

> How can I redeem this wretched humdrum? . . . How can I escape from the prison of this routine? . . . Wasn't I already deeply entangled in the pettiness of everyday cares, when it first dawned on me that I must not allow myself to be suffocated under the weight of earthly routine? . . . I myself have dug the rut. . . . My days don't make me dull—it's the other way around. . . . I realize that we gradually get tired of the feverish activity that seems so important to a young mind and heart.[1]

Perhaps accumulated age and wisdom help many women to seriously think through their priorities, to push away the feverish activity that seemed so important in their younger years. Maybe it's the wretched humdrum and the weight of routine that wakes us up to stop and think about the really important things of life. Perhaps it is the entanglement of the petty everyday cares that stirs a woman's heart to number her days and think carefully about how best to fill them.

I meet so many women today who, like Janice, are trying to be Superwoman. They want to do everything, and do it all perfectly. They involve themselves in meaningless projects, spending hours like precious gold on things that have little eternal significance. Sadly, many women never stop to ask themselves *why* they work so hard, and *why* they tie up their time with pointless activity. It is the wise woman who takes inventory often, puts her priorities in God's order, and then disciplines herself to work His plan. It's the Proverbs 31 woman who prays for divine leadership, makes a priority list, and then works smart. Remember, her heavenly *wisdom* made her "worth far more than rubies." Certainly, this industrious woman spent ample time alone in the Quiet with God, for Scripture tells us she "speaks with *wisdom,* and *faithful instruction* is on her tongue."

True wisdom comes only from God. The Proverbs 31 woman knows it is humanly impossible to be all things to all people—her husband, her children, her boss, her parents, her sisters, her friends, her husband's boss, her children's schools, her church. Her vessel holds only so much water. Her wise heart tells her that when she continues to pour out all the time, her vessel soon runs dry. So she stops often, fills up with refreshing Living Water, and then, once again, has plenty to pour out for others. This virtuous woman knows that when she runs dry, her whole family suffers.

> Actions that lead to overwork, exhaustion, and burnout can't praise and glorify God. What God calls us to do we can do and do well. When we listen in silence to God's voice and speak with our friends in trust we will know what we are called to do and we will do it with a grateful heart.[2]

Dr. James Dobson addressed the current phenomenon of overwork and the price paid by the American family when he recently appeared on *Larry King Live.* He said,

> Families are in worse shape now [than in previous years]. . . . And [they are] steadily deteriorating. . . . There's never been a generation less cared for, less healthy and less prepared for life than this generation of kids.

Dobson told King,

> Parents are too busy for their kids, but they've got
> their hands full, because it is tougher to raise kids now
> than it was 20, 30, 40 years ago. . . . One of the biggest
> problems with families today is the fact that they're
> exhausted. They're just worn out. They don't have time
> for each other, much less their children.
>
> The two-career family, where you have both a hus-
> band and wife who are deeply committed to their own
> careers, usually [doesn't] have a whole lot left over. And
> the children are somewhere in between.[3]

Overwork is an American epidemic! Relaxed vacation time
is almost nonexistent. Most Americans work all the time, all
throughout the year. Faith Popcorn calls this American dilemma
"Vacation Starvation." She writes,

> Americans get the least amount of time off of any
> workers in the industrialized world. Consider that
> employees of small businesses—that's most of us—get an
> average of eight days off a year; our European and Austra-
> lian counterparts still get four to six weeks of paid leave.
> Add the days together, and we work two months longer
> each year than the Germans and two weeks longer than
> the allegedly industrious Japanese.[4]

If this trend continues, I wonder what will happen to the
health, children, marriages, and work habits of the next generation! Surely our children are learning priorities right now from
mothers and fathers who work too hard and have little time for
family, God, recreation, or themselves.

SOME WOMEN DON'T HAVE THE CHOICE NOT
TO WORK

Perhaps you, like many women trying to survive in today's
economy, don't have the option of whether or not to work

outside the home. You may need the money. Maybe you are paying off large debts and need to work until they are paid. Your husband may want you to work to bring in extra money for the family. You may be a single mother who must support yourself and your children. You may be married to a man who can't work (sick or handicapped or unemployed) or a man who won't work (lazy or irresponsible).

I meet so many women these days that must work outside the home because they have been divorced or abandoned by a husband. Most of these women have children, and while child support (if they receive it) helps, it doesn't cover all the expenses of a one-parent family.

It's a sad commentary on our society that so many marriages end in divorce. "Consider: Today, more than half of all marriages end in divorce."[5]

I deeply admire single mothers, and I wonder how in the world they rear children and work on their own. "My hat is off to those single mothers," says James Dobson. "They are really carrying a heavy load, trying to earn a living."[6]

These are women like my friend Loren.

THE PROBLEM WITH DIVORCE AND FINANCES

Loren was left financially hurting (as most divorced women are) after her divorce. Following a decade of marriage, Loren's husband met another woman, whom he married after he left Loren and his two young boys. He pays minimal monthly child-support to them. Loren and the boys moved out of the family home and into a small, cheap apartment. When they could no longer afford the rent, they found an even smaller, cheaper apartment.

Loren works two jobs in order to keep the bills paid. She never takes vacation days. She often counts coins to buy weekly groceries for her growing boys. When her older son turned eighteen, his child-support check stopped. Loren worries about her boys, their college educations, their health-insurance needs, their futures. On their peach-fuzzed faces, they still carry the pain of their father's abandonment; they still wonder why he left them, and they've had a tough time growing up without him. For many years Loren has been both mother and father, and the work and stress have taken a definite toll on her health and frame of mind.

> Wade Horn, president of the National Fatherhood Initiative, says children who grow up outside of a two-parent home "do worse on just about every measure of child well-being." The evidence is clear: The cost of marital failure is paid by all of society, not just the couple whose marriage is shattered. And yet—as Oklahoma Gov. Frank Keating put it, it's easier to get out of a marriage than a Tupperware contract.[7]

Divorce is too easy in the United States, especially since no-fault divorce laws hit our society. It sends many moms out into the workforce when they would rather be home with their children.

No-fault divorce laws give people legal encouragement to treat their marriage vows like piecrust—easily made, easily broken. Maggie Gallagher writes in her book *The Abolition of Marriage*, "For 30 years no-fault divorce laws have taught the American people that marriage is merely a temporary arrangement— one that can be dissolved at the whim of either party."[8]

Gallagher also reveals, "Eighty percent of divorces are unilateral, sought by just one spouse."[9]

For the first time in our nation, new census data shows:

Less than a quarter of the households in the United States are made up of married couples with their children. . . . The number of single-parent families [is] growing much faster than the number of married couples. . . . Households with children headed by single mothers, which account for nearly 7 percent of all households, increased by 25 percent in the 1990s.[10]

Single moms with children are typically poorer than two-parent families. Families headed by women with children "grew nearly five times faster in the 1990s than the number of married couples with children, a trend that some family experts and demographers describe today as disturbing."[11]

Divorce is also highly responsible for the scores of older women who must go back to work in order to financially support themselves.

Louis Uchitelle writes in the *New York Times,*

Hundreds of thousands of women in their 60s, part of the surge of divorces that started a generation ago, are finding themselves forced to stay in the work force because they lack sufficient money to retire. Wages in effect are becoming their pensions.[12]

Uchitelle contends that women alone in old age have always been at greater risk of falling into poverty than have married women. Nevertheless, he reasons,

Until recently, women alone generally meant widows, who at least had the pensions and savings their husbands had left them, and a tradition of living with children. Widows greatly outnumbered older divorced women until the late 1990s, but now for the first time the divorced outnumber widows.[13]

Many of these older working women are mothers and grandmothers who have worked for a lifetime both inside and outside the home. Many have spent years rearing children. After decades of marriage, divorce has either caused them to continue, by necessity, their employment, and forego retirement, or it has pushed them back into the fast-paced workforce. This is especially true when divorce settlements remove a woman's name from her husband's health insurance and give her no entitlement to any future pension.

As a result of the various pressures, the labor force participation rates of women in their early 60s—covering those holding jobs or hunting for them—rose to a record 40.1 percent last year [2000] from 32.6 percent in 1981, and there has been a similar steady rise among women in their late 60s.[14]

Women like Loren must work outside the home. Their choices are limited. They don't have the luxury of asking themselves the question "Why am I working?" They know the answer all too well.

For single women, single moms, divorced older women, and other women who feel they have no choice but to work outside the home, there are ways to carve out time for rest and reflection and personal prayer and worship. We'll talk about some of those ways throughout the pages of this book.

However, for other women, whether or not to work difficult jobs outside the home *is* a choice they can make. Some mothers discover that the extra cost of transportation, child care, work clothes, lunches out, etc., eat up most of the profit they might make working a job. After they put pencil to paper, they simply decide that taking a job isn't profitable or worth the extra work, expense, and physical stress.

WORKING FOR OTHER REASONS

Lest you think I am telling all working women to quit their outside employment, please understand what I am saying. I have women friends who love their jobs! They enjoy their work outside the home. And, for them, I thank God that each woman can choose her life's vocation and pursue it. Women are making a profound difference in this world because they can follow their passions and work hard. But most hardworking women who hold demanding jobs will tell you that they have had to seriously sort through their priorities in life. They will be the first ones to tell other women that choosing outside employment means letting some other things go. They have each struggled to find that workable balance between job and family, rest and activity, personal devotional time and meaningful time for others.

When our bodies are tired and need rest, we must step off the treadmill and rest them! If we continue to push ourselves, stay on the treadmill, and run even faster in order to accomplish the many tasks that lay ahead of us, we damage our health and our lives. Look at your own schedule. Do you find that you work far too hard? Do you have too many demands on your shoulders each and every day? Has your spiritual life, work performance, and family life grown stale and burdensome from strict, inflexible daily routines? Each day brings the same work, work, work. Is your body weary? Women today can so easily fail to stop and give their exhausted bodies a deep, relaxing, satisfying rest. In fact, most women I meet have forgotten what "rest" means. They are "rotting in the rut" and heavy routine of everyday life and work, and they are tired of it.

"Our lives often seem like overpacked suitcases bursting at the seams. In fact, we are almost always aware of being behind schedule."[15]

Meet Nancy

Before we leave this chapter, let me introduce you to my friend Nancy. She leads the average, typical life of today's wife and mother. She has a busy husband and two little boys. She works full time as a contracted professor at a prestigious college. She is proud of her position. She thinks it gives her the status her self-esteem needs. She worked long and hard to earn the necessary degrees needed to acquire a competitive teaching position. In a social context, when someone introduces her to a stranger, she beams when they say, "Nancy is a college professor."

The income isn't great, and sometimes she actually spends more on work-related expenses than she makes teaching. But Nancy will never give up her job. She believes that her busy professorial position gives her self-worth and importance. Nancy admits that without her job her self-esteem would plummet.

For the Nancys of this world: "Busyness has become a sign of importance. Having much to do, many places to go, and countless people to meet gives us status and even fame."[16]

And what a price Nancy pays for this false sense of self-esteem!

I yearn to tell Nancy,

> God has to be the source of your self-esteem and how you view yourself as a woman. Looking to another human being, or to a cultural movement . . . [or anything else!] . . . for your inner peace and sense of worth will always result in disappointment.[17]

Walk with me through one of Nancy's typical weekdays. She rises early, dresses, makes breakfast for the family, makes sack lunches for the kids. She rushes out the door, buckles her boys into seat belts, and drives them to school. She fights morning rush traffic to arrive at her job on time. She teaches a demanding course load, picks up her children from school, and stops for groceries on the way home. Then she cooks supper, washes clothes, cleans up the kitchen, and straightens the house. After she helps her children with homework, grades her own students' papers, lays out the children's clothes for the next morning, makes a few phone calls, and pays some bills, she collapses into bed. By that time she is exhausted, but is still expected to have some kind of meaningful relationship and conversation with her overworked husband—who is also exhausted.

On Saturdays, Nancy shops for more groceries, children's clothes, school supplies, and the occasional gift. She cooks, cleans house, and occasionally entertains friends for meals. She catches up on everything that didn't get attention during the week. Sometimes Nancy and her husband will hire a baby-sitter and spend an evening with friends over dinner. Sometimes they are obligated to attend evening meetings or university social events. On Sundays, Nancy rises early, gets the kids fed and dressed for church, cooks lunch and supper, and spends her Sunday evenings readying clothes, home, and lecture notes for the Monday morning work schedule.

Nancy is always physically tired. She wears bags under her eyes like glasses. She has little personal or devotional time. She rarely gets to spend meaningful time with her kids, husband, or friends. She is always running. She has no time to get sick, much less put her feet up and rest. When she stops even for a moment, she falls behind in her work and home schedule. Life holds little for Nancy except work and exhaustion and routine. She long ago lost her joy of living. She used to enjoy teaching and her students. Now she strives to get through one more day. She continues pushing and working her weary body—day after day, week after week, month after month, year after year. Nancy says she has considered taking a leave of absence from her teaching, but she knows that teaching positions are hard to find, and if she steps out of her position, she might not be able to step back into it. She knows her self-esteem would suffer, since her self-worth is so wrapped up in her academic title and position.

I know other women like Nancy who have confused their personal worth with their professional work. They think they are what they do. They think employment gives them their personal significance. They identify themselves with their work. In their own eyes, they are important and significant only because of the work they perform.

> In our production-oriented society, being busy, having an occupation, has become one of the main ways, if not the main way, of identifying ourselves. Without an occupation, not just our economic security but our very identity is endangered.[18]

I long to tell women today that their identity, their self-worth, has nothing to do with their work. It's great to be recognized as a college professor or medical doctor or lawyer or office manager or any number of work roles available to women. But for Christian women, who have entrusted their lives to Christ, personal identity and self-worth come from Him alone. Women are special individuals because God has made them in His image. Our Father loves His daughters. To be loved by God should be enough self-worth to overflow our cup of need!

"Our worth derives from God's love for us, His choice of us, His image in us (as humans). . . . Believers rarely realize the only valid concept of self-worth—Christ in us, and us in His image."[19]

For the Christian woman, personal worth comes not from who she is (her role, her title, her employment status) but from Whose she is. Only Christ can give a woman the valid concept of self-worth.

WOMEN LEAVING THE MARKETPLACE

An interesting phenomenon is taking place among working women in our society today. We women are realizing that we are tired. We are asking tough questions about our lives and our priorities. Some of us are deciding that it's just not worth the price we are paying physically, mentally, and spiritually, to bring in the extra money we earn. We want to step out of the rat race. We don't want to be Superwoman anymore. We want some free time, time to ourselves, time to take a long hot bath instead of a quick shower. We want to spend more time in prayer and Bible study and devotional readings. We want to "have a life" apart from our employment.

"The workforce of women 24 to 35 years of age is actually declining for the first time in 30 years," states *Fortune* magazine.[20]

Why? For these primary reasons:

First, women realize they have only a certain number of hours in each day. Work outside the home, work inside the home, a marriage relationship, and the rearing of children each take tremendous amounts of time. They simply can't do all their jobs well. "Most of the working mothers we interviewed said one of their major frustrations was the difficulty of trying to balance being a good mother with being a good employee," writes Larry Burkett. "Too often their priorities conflicted."[21] More and more women these days are opting to stay at home with their children. For some, it means a serious tightening of the family's financial belt, driving less-expensive cars, buying cheaper clothes, sending their children to public instead of private schools. But these women believe they have made the right choice for themselves and for their family.

Second, women in our society are finding that at the end of the week they have little extra money to show for all their extra work efforts.

> The sad truth is that most working mothers sacrifice time with their families with little or nothing to show for it. Most of the average working mother's wages are consumed by taxes, transportation, childcare costs, and clothing. Even when a working mother's income is large enough to substantially add to the family's budget, the surplus is often consumed by an expanded lifestyle.[22]

Third, women today realize that "the decision to leave a paying job and return home is clearly going against the tide of our society."[23] Yet these same women are sincerely tired of the physical exhaustion and personal (as well as family) chaos that a job brings. They want time to rest, to enjoy their children, to nurture their husband and marriage, to dig out of the daily dog-eat-dog work and traffic. Even so, they wonder what their co-workers and friends will say. "Isn't working a high-power corporate job a privilege?" they ask. Some women fear they will lose status in the church or community if they leave their workplaces. One friend of mine, who decided to step out of the working world, said she no longer felt comfortable in her "Professional Women"

Sunday school class! Yes, even churches can make women feel like diminished people. When looking at the sign on the Sunday school door, one friend of mine (who worked inside and not outside the home) asked me: "If this class is for 'professional' women, what does that make me? 'Unprofessional'?"

Fourth, Christian women are discovering that they need a certain amount of time each day to maintain their spirits. They want unhurried time with God. They want to study their Bible. They want to sit in a quiet room and read a spiritually deep book. Women need time to think and ponder and reflect and grow in their faith. Women today are working so hard and so many hours that they are withering spiritually. "More women than ever are seeking to leave full-time jobs and return home to become stay-at-home moms!"[24]

Their choices shouldn't surprise us!

THINKING THROUGH OUR PRIORITIES

On the one hand, we are fortunate to have so many vocational choices in this present society. Women in the past haven't had the educational and job opportunities that we have today.

On the other hand, more choices mean we have more decisions to make about those choices. Making decisions about work and employment often prove difficult. When a Christian woman decides to discontinue employment and have more time for herself and her family, she will find that she must carefully control her involvement in other activities. It's not only employment that can eat away our personal, family, and prayer time. Community charities, schools, and churches can quickly consume our precious time with their unending (and often unnecessary) requests for our participation. We must make our priority lists even when we are stay-at-home women. Otherwise we will allow others to deplete our time and energy as much as (or more than) a full-time job would.

More and more, however, our nation is watching working

women make tough decisions to "go against the tide of society," give away their briefcases and Palm Pilots, admit they need time for their top priorities, and leave outside jobs. For women who must work, such as single women, moms, widows, and those financially overextended, many are rethinking exhausting work habits, finding alternatives to eight hours at the office and congested commutes, and meeting with financial planners who help them plan futures without employment.

It's about time.

Chapter Seven

STRESS ATTACK!

M odern people lack silence," suggests Dr. Paul Tournier. "They no longer lead their own lives; they are dragged along by events. It is a race against the clock."[1]

This "race against the clock" has produced an epidemic in the United States—the sad state of "dis-stress."

What is stress? It's certainly not a new problem. Reams have been written over the years about stress and its effects on the human body. Stress can be good or bad. Good stress (*eu-stress*) gets us out of bed in the mornings and helps us start our day. Bad stress (*dis-stress*), in overwhelming portions, can put us back into bed and make us sick.

The late Dr. Wayne E. Oates, my friend and seminary professor, explained,

> Stress is like heat in your body or in the engine of your automobile. Some of it is vitally necessary to the proper function of your body or your car. Too little or too much is equally threatening. An effective balance must be maintained.[2]

We have become a society of stressed-out women, women

who juggle too many plates in the air at the same time, women who are overwhelmed by everyday stress, women who have failed to find that "effective balance" between work and rest. (Dr. Oates coined the popular word *workaholic* to describe those people who work too much.)

Anne Morrow Lindbergh wrote in 1965,

> The world is rumbling and erupting in ever-widening circles around us. The tensions, conflicts and sufferings even in the outermost circle touch us all. . . . Modern communication loads us with more problems than the human frame can carry.[3]

If Lindbergh thought the human frame too weak to carry "modern communications, tensions, conflicts, and sufferings" almost forty years ago, what would she think of life today? Overstress in the twenty-first-century has become almost unbearable! And it is hurting us now more than ever before.

CRISIS STRESS

Crisis stress happens when we face an unexpected accident or emergency. We discover hidden physical strengths we didn't know we had. This rugged inner power springs to heart and soul and fortifies us physically when we must face and endure life's crises. When my father died, I watched my mother become a tower of strength. With focused energy she arranged a funeral, comforted remaining family members, and took care of reams of necessary paper work. She knew what had to be done, and she took it on with some mysterious innate ability.

Newscasters routinely tell us of women who perform supernatural feats of strength and power and sheer will when they face a severe crisis. We honor people who exhibit extraordinary strength and courage in times of disaster, like that shown during and after terrorists destroyed the World Trade Centers on September 11, 2001.

As you and I are faced with life's crises, we find that we can usually deal with a house fire or a tornado or a car wreck or a loved one's death when it happens suddenly. These out-of-the-ordinary events pull from our hidden strengths. These are our reserve physical powers that ordinarily lie untapped unless they are confronted with catastrophe.

Newlywed Patricia Van Tighem discovered her rich source of inner physical strength when on a sunny day in 1983, during a hike in the Canadian Rockies, she and her husband, Trevor, were attacked by a grizzly. The female bear grabbed and mauled Trevor, tearing away part of his leg. Then she charged toward Patricia.

In her book *The Bear's Embrace,* Van Tighem describes her initial terror: "Seconds pass. Time holds still. A grizzly? I take two steps back. Where am I going? What should I do? My heart beats loud in the silent, snowy woods."

Instantly she must make a life-saving decision. "Should I fight the bear? Or should I take flight and run away from it?" In these brief few seconds of crisis stress, her body automatically prepares itself to fight or to flee. It is an innate survival reaction built into the human body by the Creator. It helps keep us alive when we face enemy threats.

She chooses to run. She remembers her terror:

> I can't outrun a bear. . . . Panic rising. How will I get past the bear? . . . My mind racing. Legs like jelly. Shaky weak. Think. . . . Take off my pack. . . . My mind whirling. Climb a tree. Grizzlies can't climb trees. Nor can I! I have to.[4]

What is happening inside her body as she faces the bear and a life-threatening situation? Her heart races and her blood pressure soars to increase the flow to her brain. She has a life-and-death decision to make, and the extra blood to her head will improve her decision-making faculties. Her blood sugar rises, furnishing her with more fuel for physical energy. Blood from her gut will be ordered to the large muscles of her arms and legs. She will need increased speed and strength to either fight the bear or run from it. The blood arranges quicker clotting in case the bear tears her skin or causes her to hemorrhage internally.

Within seconds her body supplies her with extraordinary strength and sends her scurrying up a tree, groping higher and higher until she reaches thin branches. Her whole body physically prepares her to run and climb and avoid this dangerous encounter.

All this time, her mind races:

> I freeze. Terror fills me. [The bear] is right there. Eye contact. . . . [It is] charging the tree. A scream, loud. . . . Everything so fast. . . . I'm frozen.[5]

Unfortunately, this grizzly *can* climb a tree. The bear grabs her, throws her to the ground, and wraps its massive jaws around her head. Then the bear begins to chew. It gnaws her head, she remembers, "like a dog chews a bone." After the savage attack, she lies on the ground, bleeding, broken, and barely breathing. Both Patricia and Trevor suffer numerous physical injuries. They spend the next decade of their lives together enduring multiple surgeries, physical therapy, severe pain, and facial disfigurement.

When you and I, like Patricia and Trevor, experience crisis stress—such as a bear attack or a child's suicide or the sudden death of a spouse or a devastating hurricane—we usually have family, friends, church members, and even strangers who rush to our aid. They stand by our side, physically helping us, praying with us, caring for our children, cleaning our house, arranging necessary funerals, building and reconstructing damaged property. (Patricia and Trevor had many family members and friends who came immediately to their assistance.)

People expect us to suffer intense stress, to the point of collapse, when tough events suddenly hit us. We give ourselves permission to take the needed time to mend, heal, grieve, and rebuild. Everyone understands the reason we are failing to cope well with life at that particular time. They expect us to need love and care, time and space to recover from our losses. They give hands-on physical help to bring us through crisis stress. Most people have, themselves, experienced tragedy. They know, only too well, how life's inevitable catastrophes can knock us off our feet.

But consider this: The everyday, small, repeating stresses of life can also knock us off our feet! These daily aggravations—our "races against the clock"—can make us sick. They can quickly accumulate on top of each other and become deadly to our physical health.

THE PROBLEM OF EVERYDAY STRESS

Did you know that too much everyday, ordinary stress will make you physically ill?

> If you are operating on stress overload, you can expect to become sick. Irritating daily hassles can wear you down like a car engine racing at full throttle with the emergency brake on. You can expect to become just as ill with these repeated, daily aggravations as you would from major, life-changing traumas.[6]

Life's little irritations—those constant daily hassles—can produce the same physical responses for survival as those we discover when we encounter a grizzly bear! The mind becomes alert. The heart races and sends extra blood to the muscles. The alerted muscles flex with extra strength.

In the above crisis-stress encounter—the bear attack—the grizzly strikes and then leaves. However, in everyday stress—those troublesome daily hassles—the "grizzly" stays. The bear continues to frighten us and to threaten our lives. Our mind, heart, and muscles stay on continual alert. They remain at complete attention, armed and ready to fight or flee from the enemy. The "enemy," though, never goes away. Day after day after day, overstress keeps us in anticipation of the bear's attack as we cling to thin branches at the top of the tree. We live every day of our lives with our body screaming out, "Okay! Call it quick! Do I fight or do I flee?!"

These wonderful life-saving physical stress responders deal well with the occasional bear attack. Yet the stress that plagues women today is not generally a dangerous confrontation with a wild beast, but "rather a host of emotional threats like getting stuck in traffic and fights with customers, co-workers, or family members, that often occur several times a day."[7] Our bodies prepare physically for a temporary attack, but without relief, these fight-or-flight responses "are now not only not useful but potentially damaging and deadly. Repeatedly invoked, it is not hard to see how they can contribute to hypertension, strokes, heart attacks, diabetes, ulcers, neck or low back pain and other 'diseases of civilization.' "[8]

When we can find no relief from these everyday stresses, they tend to multiply. We become touchy with our husband. We respond more adversely to the little annoyances caused by our kids. We become overly frustrated with ourselves. The least added stress—such as a "simple criticism" from a loved one (if there is such a thing!)—can send us crashing into tears.

Paul Brand writes,

> When we are under severe strain, maybe resulting from an *accumulation of small stresses*—bills, work pressures, irritating habits of family members—suddenly *every minor frustration hits like a blow*. We have become hypersensitive, and our minds are telling us we need a respite as surely as neuronal hypersensitivity warns our bodies of a need for relief.[9]

Medical science has known for years what the "accumulation

of small stresses" can do to our bodies. Doctors have linked over-stress to "the development and course of cancer, high blood pressure, heart attacks, diabetes, asthma, allergies, ulcers, colitis, alcoholism, smoking, obesity, headaches, backaches and many other diseases."[10]

Is it any wonder that heart disease is the number-one killer of women over thirty-five in the United States today? Heart disease now kills five times as many women as breast cancer.[11]

Dr. Michele Hamilton, associate clinical professor of cardiology at UCLA, informs us, "Heart disease has long been considered an illness of men. In fact, it is more prevalent in women. More than 500,000 women die each year from heart attacks and strokes."[12]

Overstressed women are at risk for all stress-related diseases!

The everyday stresses of "bills, work pressures, and irritating habits of family members," as well as many other things, are like a steady drip on a rock. Drip, drip, drip—and soon the multiplied drops of water will wear away the solid stone. When we endure the continual drip, drip, drip of daily agitations, those everyday, unending stresses will overwhelm us and hurt our health.

As hard as it is to believe, the stacking up of everyday stresses, day after day, can be just as hazardous to our health as a major catastrophe!

> Most researchers today accept that major stressful events do indeed take a toll on health. But the latest research suggests that the average person is as likely to be "nibbled to death" by *everyday hassles* as overwhelmed by tragedies.[13]

Do you feel "nibbled to death by everyday hassles"? Do you feel dragged along by events that seem out of your control? Consider the old adage that asks, "How do you eat an elephant? One bite at a time." A constant, unrelenting "nibble" of stress—if allowed to—can eat up the strongest, most determined woman. Susan Forward writes,

> There is ample evidence that the mind, emotions and body are intimately connected. Emotional distress can significantly increase our vulnerability to headaches, muscle spasms, gastrointestinal problems, respiratory disorders and a host of other ailments.[14]

While women today experience "nibbling" dis-stress at home or in Wal-Mart checkout lines or around the Christmas table with bickering in-laws or in stop-still traffic jams, they complain most often about the dis-stress they endure in the marketplace—job stress.

Chapter Eight

JOB STRESS

Much of an employed women's everyday stress is brought on in the workplace. This is especially true for the working mother who holds down a full-time job, helps her husband, and rears her children. The stress multiplies when the working mother is single and must financially support and raise her children alone. On the average, working moms work too hard, labor too many hours in a single day, get minimal sleep at night, and have little or no occasion to rest during the day. Today's working mother is sleep-starved, and she is at high risk for stress-related diseases.

What is job stress? The experts tell us that work pressures are far and away the leading source of stress for American adults. Job stress has been steadily increasing over the past few decades. Some recent studies show:

- Forty percent of workers reported their job was very or extremely stressful.
- Twenty-five percent view their jobs as the number-one stressor in their lives.
- Eighty percent of workers feel some major stress on the job.

- More people complain about job stress than about their health, finances, or family problems!

"A 1992 United Nations Report labeled job stress 'the 20th-Century Disease,' and a few years later the World Health Organization said it had become a 'Worldwide Epidemic.' "[1]

"*Time* magazine's June 6, 1983, cover story called stress 'The Epidemic of the Eighties,' and referred to it as *our leading health problem*! There can be little doubt that the situation has progressively worsened since then. Numerous surveys confirm that adult Americans perceive they are under much more stress than a decade or two ago."[2]

"Work daze"—a new expression for all those overworked Americans—has now joined our vocabulary. Faith Popcorn says,

> Increasing overtime is putting unprecedented pressure on workers, forcing many of them to work long hours without adequate sleep. . . . Drowsy workers are a danger to others. . . . James Maas, a psychology professor at Cornell, says that 100 million Americans, 40 percent of the population, are severely sleep deprived.[3]

How can someone's sleep deprivation be a danger to others? Imagine undergoing serious surgery performed by a drowsy doctor. Or having a sleepy pharmacist fill your medical prescription. Do you want an exhausted carpool mom driving your youngsters to preschool? Our very lives depend on those in society who should be well-rested and alert—airplane pilots, truck and bus drivers, dentists, firemen, police officers, nurses, bank tellers, and many others. "Forty percent of the population are severely sleep deprived"?! One only needs to read the daily newspaper or turn on the evening news to see the suffering toll on human life when people work too hard and sleep too little. Everyday stress, produced by overwork and lack of adequate rest, puts all Americans at deadly risk.

Yet in our society, "work is fast becoming the American

Christian's major source of identity," writes Charles Swindoll. "The answer to most of our problems (we are told) is '*work harder*.' "[4]

Indeed, many women *do* identify who they are by the work they do. Society's push to "work harder" leads to working longer hours. Working longer hours leads to inadequate sleep and rest. Dr. Swindoll makes an interesting point when he reminds us that not only does society urge us to work harder, but the church can add even more pressure on its members to increase workloads. He writes that some people believe: "You aren't really serving the Lord unless you consistently push yourself to the point of fatigue." It's the old burn-out-rather-than-rust-out line.[5]

When we try to fulfill everything expected of us by our society, our church, our families, our bosses, our co-workers, and others, we become super-sensitive, exhausted, energy-depleted, and sleep-deprived women! We see these overworked, dis-stressed, and dazed women everywhere . . . in the workplace, in the supermarket, in the home, and even in the church.

John Eldredge suggests,

> Walk into most churches in America, have a look around, and ask yourself this question: What is a Christian woman? . . . Don't listen to what is said, look at what you find there. There is no doubt about it. You'd have to admit a Christian woman is . . . *tired*. All we've offered the feminine soul is pressure to "be a good servant."[6]

When working mothers are "dragged along by events" and feel the pressures and stresses of overwork, the result can be burn-out. Not only do women today feel *physical* burnout but they are also experiencing *emotional* burnout. As we have seen, many working moms consider the physical hardship of employment to be equal or less than the emotional dis-stress they experience.

Among . . . working mothers, tales abound of guilt; of the inability to juggle the demands of work, children, a husband and a home without being fatigued and feeling inadequate.[7]

Diane Passno observes, "Guilt is very common for women who feel they don't quite measure up to what it means to be a 'Proverbs 31 Woman.' "

Passno agrees with John Eldredge when she writes,

I think our churches often play a role in the "guilt trip" because of the requirements and expectations demanded of women in congregations. There is a not-so-subtle message that often equates salvation with duty to church, and women find themselves leaving hearth and home to meet these expectations that often make their lives far more difficult. . . . When they [church roles and jobs] are mandatory and there is no flexibility, a woman can easily be overwhelmed and completely frazzled by the expectations placed upon her shoulders.[8]

It's a fact. Overwork, fatigue, expectations from others, and feelings of inadequacy—all contributing to unrelenting everyday stress—can make a woman sick.

"One [person] reacts to increased tension with a headache, another with high blood pressure, and still another with sleeplessness, irritability, and depression," writes Karl Menninger. "The repetition of minor irritations and frustrations may be cumulative in their effects to a *disturbing degree*."[9]

Everyday stress sends America's women by the droves to doctors' offices for medical help. One stress study shows that "from 75 to 90 percent of all visits to primary-care physicians are for stress-related disorders."[10]

OTHER TYPES OF EVERYDAY STRESS

Another deadly stressor that occurs daily for many working women is the commute to and from the workplace. Perhaps you too endure a long difficult commute by car, train, bus, or subway. I can well remember the stress caused by commuting at least two hours a day from my home to my office in downtown Boston. I found it exhausting. Jack Niles calls the stress caused by common commuting "commute cancer."

> [Commute cancer] describes all the harmful effects of commuting, including the stress, the lost productivity, the stolen family time. With commutes getting longer, as sprawl forces families to move farther from central cities, commute cancer is getting worse.[11]

For the hours you spend commuting each day, you are bombarded with traffic noise, road rage, tension, and potential accidents. It's no wonder that many women are physically exhausted and emotionally tense by the time they arrive at work. After a full day of overwork and long hours, a woman must still face the difficult commute back to her home. Whether she drives, takes the train, subway, or bus, the tension and tiredness brought about by after-work commute pressures can take a definite toll on family life that evening.

However difficult women may find outside employment ("work daze"), as well as getting back and forth to work ("commute cancer"), most women tell me that keeping up a home—including housework, house repair, and yard work—causes just as much stress as outside employment! Keeping a house running properly requires huge amounts of energy and resourcefulness. It's a full-time job in itself.

Home and family record-keeping is stressful. Many married women I know take on this vital role in their households. Most single moms have no choice but to handle record-keeping themselves. Record handlers must keep up with car payments, house mortgages, utility expenses, life- and car- and house-insurance payments, retirement accounts, social security benefits, medical insurance premiums, checking and saving accounts—the list goes on and on. They pay the bills, pay repairmen, and prepare the income tax forms.

Employment, commute, housework, and the rigors of routine record-keeping can keep a woman overwhelmed.

And to this workload, many women add parenting and grandparenting. Children bring big blessings to our lives—there's no doubt about it. I have two "big blessings" of my own! But children also bring huge amounts of additional work to our daily schedules. Many women today, who have already "emptied" their nests of their own children, are now taking on the responsibility of raising their grandchildren. Women are also discovering that full-grown children, who have already left the nest, often fly back to live there! They move right back into their own childhood bedrooms. Sometimes they even bring a wife and children!

Of course we love our children and our grandchildren! We welcome their visits! We cherish our times together! They are truly God's gifts to us. But additional family members mean additional meals to prepare, clothes to launder, bills to pay, groceries to buy—more physical work and less physical rest.

Women today also must deal with out-of-the-ordinary stress issues. Consider women caught in the "sandwich" generation. At the same time they are raising teenagers, they are also taking care of aging and/or ill parents. They are teaching their teens to drive while making sure their parents take the correct medications. They are dealing with their child's dating dilemmas as well as transporting elderly in-laws to doctor's appointments and sleeping next to hospital beds.

Most women handle their everyday stressors well. They keep up, make an honest effort to get everything done, and cope adequately with common everyday hassles. But then life throws a curveball. They get sick or need surgery. Someone they love and care for becomes ill, has a stroke, or lands in the hospital. Or . . . their teenage daughter gets pregnant; their married daughter births a severely handicapped baby; their husband retires early from his job; their son divorces his wife; an unexpected house repair or medical expense eats away at family finances. Just when we feel we are handling everything, and we think we are doing a fairly good job, *change* comes along, adds overwhelming stress, and we wonder how in the world we will cope.

Researcher George Barna, in his book *Boiling Point,* writes, "Nothing is exempt from *change* these days; everything, it seems, is up for grabs, almost every day."

Barna says current surveys reveal that Americans are the most stressed-out people on earth. Why?

> Largely due to the range and degree of instability and uncertainty we constantly juggle. . . . There is a high probability that if you lead a normal life (whatever that is), during a single day you will have to negotiate at least one significant emotional, intellectual, moral, spiritual, finan-cial, relational or physical *change* that has never previously emerged in your life.[12]

Sometimes we can anticipate these "emotional, intellectual, moral, spiritual, financial, relational, and physical" changes that occur. When my friend Sandy was told by her two pregnant daughters and one pregnant daughter-in-law that she could expect three little red newborns to come the same spring, Sandy anticipated a dramatic life change. She spent most of winter get-ting ready for the next year's new deliveries. When they came, she expected them. Anticipated change brings less stress than unexpected change, especially when change comes on top of change. When changes come too closely together, however, they can leave even the most organized woman overwhelmed.

"Not only is change inevitable, occurring at a blistering pace and invading every dimension of our lives, but also the pace of change is accelerating at what seems to be a geometric rate."[13]

Some years ago two scientists, Drs. Holmes and Masuda, completed what they called a "Social Readjustment Rating

Scale." In this scale, they listed forty-three major and minor life changes and gave each a certain number of points. They concluded that if at any given time a person's total points adds up to three hundred or more, she should stop and take note, for she is overstressed and in danger of becoming sick.

For instance, if you have just lost a spouse to death, Holmes and Masuda gives that stress-change the highest point total—100. A divorce is rated at 73 points. A jail term registers at 63 points. They end their list with "minor violations of the law," which bring 11 points. After looking at the "Social Readjustment Rating Scale" and assessing your life over the last year, you can count up the total points and see the level of stress you are currently coping with.*

We are constantly surrounded by certain stressors—dis-stress that can overwhelm us and break us. It's just part of the fast-paced American lifestyle we live.

"It . . . seems as if our society were designed to break the human spirit," writes Arthur Gish in his book *Beyond the Rat Race.* "Rather than a style of life, it might be called a style of death."[14]

Whether a "style of life" or a "style of death," whether a bear attack or an unexpected divorce, whether "commute cancer" or "work daze," whether expected change or unexpected change, whether stress caused by ourselves or stress caused by others, I pray that you and I both can maintain a personal health watch and avoid becoming victims of dis-stress.

---

*I have included the "Social Readjustment Rating Scale" by Holmes and Masuda on pages 140–142.

Chapter Nine

MAJORING IN THE MINORS

Not long ago I read about a police rescue in Zephyrhills, Florida. Police Captain Richard Scudder received a frantic phone call: A shopper had spotted a newborn baby left unattended in a locked Dodge Caravan in Wal-Mart's parking lot. It was an unusually hot afternoon, and officer David Feger rushed to the scene. Looking inside, he saw the apparently lifeless infant wrapped in a blanket and strapped into a car seat. The child was not breathing.

Taking immediate action, Feger struggled to open the van door with a "Slim Jim." When that didn't work, he shattered the window with his metal baton. Hoping the child was still alive, he reached inside and touched the unconscious infant.

That's when he discovered that the "unconscious infant" was a plastic doll!

Later the officers had a few laughs. They paid the startled van's owner $243 to fix the broken window. And they got back to work.

We can smile about the incident and agree that the police did the right thing. Too many babies have, indeed, died in sweltering cars. But perhaps we can learn something also. Maybe it contains a deeper lesson for society today—a lesson about what happens when we major on the minors in life.[1]

Life has become increasingly complicated in the past few decades. Nothing is simple anymore. If we aren't always on guard, we can quickly fill our days with insignificant activities, projects, and goals that rescue plastic dolls from locked vans in Wal-Mart parking lots, but don't accomplish any worthwhile purpose. Society has grown so fast-paced that even we Christian women can fail to give ourselves needed time to ponder life, to question our purpose, to seek God's will. For instance, when was the last time we stopped and asked ourselves a major question of faith: "What is the meaning of this short life?"

"Our busy, fast-paced American culture has no time for such a question," writes Thaddeus Barnum. "Our schedules are jam-packed. We don't even have time for ourselves. We're pulled in every direction just to make ends meet."

Barnum is right on target when he writes about today's American busy-ness:

> Today, both parents work full-time jobs, and children are left to grow up without their constant presence. For some of us, it's worse. We're faced with the burden of being separated and single. We are left with the mounting guilt of not being present for our kids, stress at work, financial demands, social pressure from friends, and the inner demands—challenging and never ending—to be successful, attractive, pulled together, and in control. . . . We don't take time to think, dream, read the Bible, pray, and wonder about the meaning of life—especially our life.[2]

I meet so many women who allow their days to become super-stressful, who stay far too busy, who hurry too much, and who spend their precious prime-time hours majoring in the minors of life. They don't do it intentionally. It's just that we can get so swept up in the fast-moving current of society that we forget what really is, and what really isn't, important in life. Learning not to major in the minors has been a challenge for me personally. I used to have this crazed notion that mothers could single-handedly solve all the complicated problems faced by each family member. When I finally collapsed from stress and exhaustion, broke a few teeth from nervously grinding them as I slept, and knocked my jaw out of sync, causing incredible pain, I learned something about "majors" and "minors." I finally figured out how many problems I could solve, and what problems I had to let go and be solved by other people. It helped me to slow down into more simplicity and stop hurrying like a hamster on a wheel to get done "all things for all people."

"The lives of the *hurry-sick* lack simplicity."[3] What is "hurry-sickness"? Meyer Friedman defines it:

> Above all [it is] a continuous struggle and unremitting attempt to accomplish or achieve more and more things or participate in more and more events in less and less time, frequently in the face of opposition, real or imagined, from other persons.[4]

FRONT SEAT AND BACKSEAT PRIORITIES

Secular culture constantly majors in the minors. It bills as priority the things that should take a rear seat in life.

"Our secular culture tells us that if a person wants to be acceptable she must look good, feel good, and make good," writes author Lewis Smedes.

> The self we are supposed to be comes in a svelte body, draped in designer clothes, and capped with a gorgeous face. Further, she feels fantastic about herself; she feels seductive, alive, adorable, and wholly fulfilled. To top it

off, she makes a lot of money and has considerable clout with important people.[5]

These "perfect" size-2 women parade for us across television and movie screens, smile at us from magazine ads, and make us think that clothes, money, beauty, and clout are life's *majors* to be gained at all costs.

Beauty has become an obsession in our society. The latest "look young" craze comes from a syringe full of diluted Botulinum Toxin Type A, better known as Botox. A poison injected by needle into the face, the drug temporarily paralyzes the muscles that cause wrinkles. Within days, a wrinkled forehead becomes as smooth as a young girl's—at least for a few months. These painful injections must be repeated.

Close to a million people asked for Botox last year, and millions more will want it this year. That's in addition to the millions of healthy Americans who will undergo costly surgery simply to make themselves "look better." Why are we willing to spend so much for results that are so temporary? In his book *When No One Sees: The Importance of Character in an Age of Image,* philosopher Os Guinness says, with customary insight, that it has to do with "the modern world's obsession with physical appearance."[6]

Physical attractiveness is highly desired. Some women go to great lengths to achieve and maintain physical beauty because they just aren't happy with their bodies. And their attitude about the way they look is affecting their health!

Being unhappy with your body may not seem like a big deal, but experts point out that body dissatisfaction can have far-reaching health consequences.

"It's a real public health problem," says Dr. Shari Lusskin, a clinical assistant professor of psychiatry at New York University School of Medicine. "Women who become obsessively preoccupied with their body image can resort to self-destructive means to maintain their body weight at or below their ideal weight."

Women with body dissatisfaction are more likely to have eating disorders, be depressed, have a lower quality of life, exercise less, and may be less likely to quit smoking, the research found.[7]

Author Nathaniel Hawthorne addresses this "beauty obsession" in his short story "The Birthmark." The tale begins with Georgiana's scientist husband, Alymer, obsessing about a small flaw on the side of his Barbie-figured, beautiful wife's face. Georgiana's birthmark compels Alymer to mix up a special potion that will rid his wife of this minor flaw. He works frantically in his lab to concoct a remedy; finally successful, he presents her with the draught. She drinks it, and it works—the birthmark fades and disappears. Alymer's triumph turns to despair, though, for soon after the mark is gone, Georgiana is overcome by the poisonous potion and dies.[8]

Not only are weight, fashion, and beauty major concerns in our society, but position and clout stand right beside them. Jesus, in Matthew 18, directly talks about how unimportant these are.

When the disciples asked Jesus who had the greatest clout and position in God's kingdom, Jesus didn't point to the rich or the beautiful or the prestigious religious leaders of His day. Jesus picked up a little child and put him on His lap. This child is the greatest in the kingdom of heaven, He said (see Matthew 18:1–4).

When a rich, important young man asked Jesus how he could obtain eternal life, Jesus in essence told him to empty his savings account, cash out his high-interest CDs, liquidate his assets, and give all his wealth away (see Matthew 19:16–23). In other words, the rich man majored in the minors [money, possessions, stocks, Calvin Klein], and forgot about the true meaning of life.

When people around Jesus worried about what they would eat or wear, Jesus told them to stop being anxious about food and clothes. They just aren't worth worrying about. A bowl of oatmeal will fill an empty stomach just as quickly as beef roast au jus. An outfit from The Salvation Army clearance store will cover your body just as completely as a Liz Claiborne designer suit. Jesus promised that God will supply everything you need (see Matthew 6:25–34).

Forget earth's false treasures, Jesus told His listeners. They are minors! They are plastic baby dolls in locked vans! Concentrate on storing up heaven's treasures—things that won't rust in your garage, things that moths won't eat in your drawers, things that won't end up in next spring's garage sale (see Matthew 6:19–24).

These things—clout, clothes, food, money, possessions— aren't major enough to spend your life earning and collecting. Repeatedly Jesus tells us what is really important. Store up heavenly treasures: "For where your treasure is, there your heart will be also" (Matthew 6:21). You can't love both God and money. You have to choose which one to love and which one to hate. God is a major. Money is a minor.

> Our treasure focuses our heart. "Your heart will be where what you treasure is," Jesus tells us (Matthew 6:21). Remember that our heart is our will, or our spirit: the center of our being from which our life flows. It is what gives orientation to everything we do. A heart rightly directed therefore brings health and wholeness to the entire personality.[9]

In other words, don't major in making meals like Emeril Lagasse (of *Emeril Live*) or about wearing the latest designer jeans. Major in seeking God. Work on that eternal relationship.

Is Jesus telling us to stop working and sit on our hands? Of course not. Jesus worked very hard during His young adult years in His father's shop. And He did His work well. In fact, second-century Christian apologist Justin Martyr said,

> During [Jesus'] lifetime it was still common to see Galilean farmers using plows made by the carpenter Jesus of Nazareth! Think about it: The second Person of the triune Godhead spent much of his earthly life working in a

woodshop. By that act alone God forever established the significance of our work in this world.[10]

Jesus also worked hard during His years of public ministry—preaching, healing, traveling. He's not telling us to stop working. Even the most humbling work we do in God's plan can glorify God. Jesus is simply telling us to crave God, not gold.

> For most of us, shedding the power that possessions and material comforts hold over us is a lifelong process and one of the most difficult. I've found that the "love of money" springs up like a noxious weed. Servitude to money and possessions demands our energies, our time, and our loyalties.[11]

Joseph Girzone, author of the popular *Joshua* series, writes, "Not that [Jesus] was condemning the possession of things, but the *distraction and the craving for them* which simulates the worship and attention we should reserve only for God."

Father Girzone warns us, "If we are not careful, craving material things can take the place of our worship of God and cause us to do things that are evil and vile in order to maintain and increase our possessions, even destroying other people in the process."

Jesus gave us His perfect example of how we are to react to earth's possessions—with a strong sense of detachment.

"Detachment from material possessions was a high priority in Jesus' approach to spirituality, and He exemplified this in His own life."[12]

Do you know women today who are spiritually hungry? They have not found the expected fulfillment in material possessions. They sense an empty place in their lives, a place only God himself can fill. Their souls are dry. Nothing the world offers them seems satisfying.

Ours is a time of intense spiritual hunger. People are

thirsting for the sacred, the mysterious, the mystical. They are looking for more than a good job, a full closet, and a balanced checkbook.[13]

The pursuit of possessions can quickly waste our days, bring us overwhelming dis-stress, and rob us of our joy. Joy comes from the Lord, not Lord & Taylor's.

When life becomes focused upon God instead of "things," one not only *is freed from* all the anxieties that attend possession, but he also is *made free to* use "things" with all the blessing and joy for which they were created and given to us in the first place.[14]

Recently I reread Guy de Maupassant's eye-opening story of Matilda, a poor French woman who longed for the world's rich treasures but who had married a simple clerk.

"She had neither frocks nor jewels, nothing. And she loved only those things," writes de Maupassant. When her husband, Loisel, brought Matilda a rare and unexpected Cabinet Ball invitation, Matilda cried, "I am vexed not to have a jewel, not one stone, nothing to adorn myself with. . . . There is nothing more humiliating than to have a shabby air in the midst of rich women!"

But Matilda had a well-to-do friend, a former schoolmate at the convent. "Go and find your friend Madame Forestier and ask her to lend you her jewels," Loisel told his wife.

From Mme. Forestier, Matilda borrowed an exquisite necklace of diamonds. Matilda "placed them about her throat . . . and remained in ecstasy before them."

The day of the ball arrived. Matilda wore the necklace. She "danced with enthusiasm, with passion, intoxicated with pleasure. . . ." But, after the ball, when Matilda and Loisel arrived home, she discovered to her horror that the necklace was no longer upon her throat. She had lost it. They searched the city for days. They had no money to pay Madame Forestier or to replace it. Finally, in desperation, Matilda and her husband borrowed, at high interest, thirty-six-thousand francs. They bought an identical diamond necklace, and Matilda returned it to her friend.

But the heavy debt cost Matilda and Loisel dearly. Matilda took hard scrubwoman jobs and worked without rest for the next ten years. Loisel took on extra tasks at night until they had finally earned enough money to repay the loan with interest. The hard labor and long hours took a toll on the couple. Matilda, once so beautiful and vibrant, now seemed old, "her hair badly dressed, her skirts awry, her hands red . . . a strong, hard woman . . . the crude woman of the poor household."

One Sunday, as Matilda took a long overdue walk in the Champs-Élysees, she came upon Mme. Forestier, "still young, still pretty, still attractive." Matilda decided to tell her friend about losing the necklace and how she had worked so hard to replace it. Mme. Forestier was shocked.

"You say that you bought a diamond necklace to replace mine?" she asked. Mme. Forestier took Matilda's hands: "Oh, my poor Matilda! Mine were false. They were not worth over five hundred francs!"[15]

Every time I read *The Necklace,* I stop and reexamine my own life, my own wants, my own desires. How often I too have found myself working hard and long hours for the "false necklaces" our culture so craves, the urge to impress that society so treasures, the empty promises brought by material possessions. Are not all our earthly "treasures" that we work so hard to possess just worthless fakes in the long run of eternity?

God offers us so much more. He gives us eternal treasures, riches that will last. How quickly we can get caught up in the rat race to acquire what society values. How easily we settle for less than what God offers us. God offers us true treasure—communion with Him, solitude, and sacred rest.

Coming to Christ in the Quiet Place is not for the purpose

of recharging our batteries in order to "enter life's many competitions with new vigor and strength." When we emerge from the Quiet Place, "we find that solitude gives us power not to win the rat race but to ignore the rat race altogether."[16] The rat race is no longer attractive to us. We've tasted a much deeper, more fulfilling happiness than society can ever offer us.

It's true. Coming to the Quiet increases our desire to give up those things that have no eternal value and to reclaim those things that have true and lasting value. It is in the Quiet Place that God whispers to us and makes us aware of life's true treasure—himself. In relationship with the living Christ, frocks and jewels entice us no longer. We realize earth's diamond necklaces hold little value to us. We regard possessions as tools to be used, not loved and adored, labored for and stored. "Get all you *can, can* all you get, and then sit on the *can*" is no longer our motto. In the Quiet Place, God helps us discover the place of possessions in our earthly lives. He helps us to drastically shift our priorities from the world to Him—to close our eyes at what the world values and to really see the gifts He offers. In the Quiet Place, God offers us the freedom of simplicity from our possessions. Simplicity is simply "a lessened evaluation of what the world promotes as important."[17]

It distresses me greatly to see how the world and its retailers are teaching our children "false necklace" values. In their competitive fight to expand their market, they are seeking out a younger, more susceptible consumer—children. Clothing retailers have upset many parents by marketing "sexy" apparel to their elementary-aged girls.

When CNN commentator Betsy Hart took her six-year-old daughter shopping, she found clothes for young girls to be "cut so tight and low, or so high and tight, that there was nothing appropriate for my little one." She found the clothes "unnecessarily sexualizing our littlest girls." . . . Clothes "getting consistently lower and tighter, flaunting 'breasts, bellies and bottoms' as never before."[18]

Charles Colson writes about Abercrombie & Fitch's latest product for seven- to fourteen-year-olds: thongs! "Rearless underwear for very young girls. . . . It's 'Frederick's of Hollywood' for kids!" states one outraged mother. Betsy Hart calls these thongs for little girls "dental floss that passes for underwear." On the thongs are written words like "Wink, Wink" and "Eye Candy."

When parents revolted against Abercrombie & Fitch, company spokesman Hampton Carney told them: "It's cute and fun and sweet. Any misinterpretation of that is purely in the eye of the beholder."

In his *BreakPoint* radio spot, Colson comments on this latest "from diaper to thong" retailer sales ploy: "Our children," he writes, "sadly enough, are going to face a lot of cultural garbage in our style-obsessed society. . . . Parents must teach their kids how to become persons of substance, how to respond properly to these insulting images by rejecting them outright and rejecting those who promote them."[19]

Our nation's little girls want to dress like Britney Spears! "I like to look sexy," one five-year-old girl told ABC News when interviewed on the subject. Provocative and sexy five-year-olds? Oh, please! What is happening to our children, our future wives and mothers? What is society teaching our children about "the meaning of this short life"? They are trying to clothe our young daughters in thongs when they should be concerned about spiritual and moral values.

"Style is a major ingredient of the emptiness in modern culture," writes social critic Os Guinness. "Thus it affects the drive to sex and violence."[20]

We now live in a society abounding in sex and violence. And our children are suffering.

Don't let the world squeeze you into its mold, Paul urges the

Romans (see Romans 12:2). We've become a "Jell-O" society, easily conformed to the world's shape, taking to heart what society most values. We need strong backs and determined wills for, as Christian mothers today, we must swim upstream against society's fast-moving tide. We must keep up our guards lest we, unawares, float downstream with the rest of an unthinking and self-flaunting culture. Swimming upstream takes strength and courage. Strength and courage come from spending time with God in the Quiet Place. "Come to Me," Jesus calls us. "Come to Me, all you who labor. . . ."

Today's Christian woman is tired and overworked, on the edge of exhaustion and burnout. How can we praise and glorify God when we are overwhelmed and dis-stressed?

As I reread the Gospels, I discover that Jesus did all the work His Father gave Him to do without becoming overwhelmed and dis-stressed. In the beautiful prayer He prayed shortly before His death, Jesus said to His Father: "I have brought you glory on earth by *completing the work you gave me to do*" (John 17:4, emphasis mine).

How I long for those to be my final words as I depart this life—"I have *completed the work you gave me to do!*" If I can't see myself saying this, perhaps it is because I am far too busy with work that God doesn't intend for me to do—unimportant work, majoring-in-the-minors work! Perhaps I don't have my priorities in God's order.

Will I ever complete the work God has given me to do? Not at this hurry-sickness pace. Not on this majoring-in-the-minors schedule. Not in this life . . . unless I heed His comforting call: "Come to Me, all you who labor. . . ."

Jesus, please show me your priorities in life! What is major? What is minor? Help me to do my work with the dedication, skill, and unhurried confidence that you had when you lived here.

With all the work Jesus had to do during His brief life on earth, Scripture never shows Jesus being in a hurry. When my kids were young, God used the child-rearing experience to teach me about being patient. I had never been much of a patient person. Oftentimes I heard myself saying to my youngsters, "Hurry, Christian!" or "Hurry, Alyce," when we really didn't need to hurry at all. It had become a habit with me—a "hurry" habit. I was rushing my kids to hurry through life when I had no reason to rush them!

Child psychologist David Elkind thinks we as a society hurry our kids into adulthood. "Hurried children grow up too fast," he writes, "pushed in their early years toward . . . achievement and exposed to experiences that tax their adaptive capacity."[21]

We are seeing "stress-related problems, usually confined to adults . . . developing in children at earlier ages. . . . Faced with adult tasks and tensions before they are prepared emotionally and psychologically, children feel bewildered and stressed."[22]

As a little girl, I loved to sit in the grass, think about life, play with my dolls, and dream about the future. I am grateful to my mother for not scheduling my after-school and weekend activities too tightly. I needed room in my young life for carefree days of silence and solitude, days when I could leisurely sit on my swing set or dress up my dog. Children today seem so overscheduled with activities. I see moms and kids in SUV's all over my neighborhood rushing to soccer practice, piano lessons, ballet practice, and karate lessons every afternoon and evening. I have often wondered when these boys and girls dream the dreams that children dream.

Jesus did His work with love and compassion, showing no irritation when people interrupted. Was it because Jesus spent considerable time in the Quiet Place with God, and that, through prayer, He came to understand His priorities? Was it that those things so important to our society—clothes, food, homes, possessions—held no interest for Jesus? Jesus wanted only to do His Father's will. He didn't desire to possess or impress. He held on to nothing except His intense love for God and His compassionate service-love for people. He didn't make New Year's resolutions. His main purpose was to praise and glorify God and to complete the work God gave Him to do. He lived a balanced life, even though He worked hard and at times hurt with hunger and exhaustion. Jesus' life wasn't easy, but He didn't spend precious time searching for His "sense of self" or for "personal fulfillment" and "happiness." These came as by-products of His intimate relationship with His Father in the Quiet Place.

I believe we can learn how to live each and every day of our lives by seriously studying how Jesus lived while on earth. Perhaps our worn-out bodies—in desperate but vain search for that illusive peace and happiness—are trying to tell us something when they become stressed-out and overwhelmed with exhaustion.

"Clearly, something is out of balance," writes John Michael Talbot, "when millions of people are wracked by stress and medicated against despair. Not that life is a picnic. Hardly. Daily living can be full of challenge and pain. But many people unnecessarily complicate their lives, and suffer from a nagging unhappiness that in some ways results directly from their own misguided search for peace and happiness."[23]

Do we "unnecessarily complicate" our lives because we do work we aren't called by God to do? Do we "suffer from a nagging unhappiness" because we spend our days frantically majoring in the minors of life? Are we leading a "misguided search for peace and happiness" because we've somehow lost our map to the Quiet Place?

"When your schedule is getting out of hand, it's a signal that it's time to slow down and reevaluate what's important rather than power through everything on the list," writes Richard Carlson.[24]

We may be afraid to reevaluate our lives in the Quiet Place, for we know that direct consultation with Jesus will change our lives. An encounter with God himself sends us scurrying from the things society holds so dear. And change is terrifying. We'd rather be safe and comfortable in our present situation. But the time always comes when we shout, "Enough of this! I can no longer stand the insignificant! I can no longer tolerate the trite!" And the time comes when we wholeheartedly agree with Karl Rahner, who honestly admits,

> My soul has become a huge warehouse where day after day the trucks unload their crates without any plan or discrimination, to be piled helterskelter in every available corner and cranny, until it is crammed full from top to bottom with the trite, the commonplace, the insignificant, the routine.[25]

Jesus clearly knew what His priorities were, for He spent a large portion of His day in communication with God in the Quiet Place. It is in the Quiet Place with the Father that we can slow down, rethink our priorities, diminish our stress, reevaluate our treasures, and decide what is really valuable in a Christian's life.

No doubt you hear, as I do, the cry of Christian women all over the country, women who are "thirsting for the sacred, the mysterious, the mystical." Women who are, indeed, "looking for more than a good job, a full closet, and a balanced checkbook." They are tired of the lifestyle that stresses their bodies and holds little value or meaning to their souls. As our society becomes more and more complicated, intense, and hurried, we will probably hear more cries from weary women—women who are fed up with frantic paces and fruitless pursuits. Women who yearn to spend time in the Quiet Place.

Let's listen carefully to their longings. Let's point them to the Quiet Place and to the One who waits there with outstretched arms.

Chapter Ten

DE-STRESSING AND RESTING OUR BODY

W e've already discussed how today's Christian woman usually works too hard, bears too many responsibilities, deals with far too much stress, and allows herself little, if any, personal time to relax. Many women race through their days at breakneck speed to work outside jobs; run an efficient household; love, support, and encourage a busy husband; and rear happy children, keeping them safe, sheltered, fed, dressed, educated, and churched. All the while, society (and sometimes even the church) tells us to work harder, accomplish more, and rest less.

Perhaps you can identify with today's Christian woman—her workload, her responsibilities, her dis-stress. If so, let's look at some practical suggestions that you and I can incorporate into our daily lives.

CONSIDER YOUR WORK OUTSIDE THE HOME

"Come to Me, all you who *labor*," Jesus said. "Labor" means to perform work under wearisome or grievous circumstances; to toil with difficulty, to exert, to strive, to take pains, to travail. Those of us who work outside the home can relate to "labor" and its meaning. As mentioned earlier, while some women can make choices about whether or not to work outside the home, many women cannot. For various reasons, they must work, and they must work hard, long hours in order to support themselves and their families. Most of the time these are single women, especially single moms who support themselves and their children with a sole income. Some women choose to work because they enjoy having extra money to buy those things that one salary can't afford. Usually these women are married, with or without children, and donate their salaries to the household's budget. Some women work because their husbands can't work, or won't work, or because their husbands ask them or expect them to work outside the home. Whatever the reason a woman embraces employment, the following practical issues are important to consider:

- What are the reasons I am working outside my home?
- Am I fulfilling someone else's expectations for me through my work?
- Do I need the money? What do I need the money for?
- Am I wise in the ways I spend the money I work hard for?
- Could I simplify my life (and/or my family's life) and choose not to work outside my home?
- Am I working physically harder than I want to work, or should work?
- Have I somehow confused my self-worth with the type of work I do?
- Does this job give me my self-esteem, or am I able to draw my self-esteem solely from God?
- Am I working so hard that I am hurting my physical health?
- Is the extra income worth the extra physical toil and risks to my health?

- Is my marriage suffering because of my job?
- Are my children suffering because of my job?
- Is my personal time with God suffering because of my job?
- Do I yearn to spend more time with God and family, but don't have time because of employment?
- What am I teaching my children about work, money, and their values?
- If I had a choice whether or not to work outside the home, which would I choose?

When we stop to look at our work habits and schedules, and truly consider their advantages and disadvantages, we can better make those decisions about our outside employment. If you must work outside your home, decide on ways to make your work more meaningful and less physically exerting. For instance:

- Do you feel "God-called" to this particular vocation or work?
- Are you working within God's plan for your life? Have you seriously prayed about your vocation in light of God's purpose for you?
- Are you doing the kind of work you enjoy, are trained to do, and find satisfying?
- Are you working because you love your job and the contributions you make to your family and community?
- Do you find your job an important outlet for your creativity?
- Would you find work elsewhere to be more fulfilling and less irritating?
- Are you taking on more responsibility than your job should require?
- Can you negotiate fewer demands and responsibilities on the job?
- Can you lessen your commute time to and from work? Or take public transportation? Or carpool?

- Can you rearrange your work hours to better benefit your and your family's schedule?
- Can you negotiate more vacation time, sick days, rest days?
- Could you use your lunch hour as a rest time? Is a quiet place available in your workplace to allow you to lie down and rest even for a few minutes during the workday?
- Financially, could you afford to work a part-time instead of a full-time job?
- If you must work, can you afford to hire some help with the housework and childcare so you can find more time to rest?
- Are you spending more time than is necessary doing jobs that might require fewer hours?
- Are you "working smart" and thereby saving valuable time?

Once again, women who work hard, both outside and inside their homes, need adequate sleep and rest time. Otherwise, they do harm to their physical bodies. God created our bodies to need regular rest and renewal, if even for a short period of time.

"There is great value in even a brief respite," writes Albert Meiburg. "If Jesus felt it necessary to go into a quiet place to recover his strength, how much more do we? Your quiet place may be a weekend getaway with your spouse. A new scene may give you stimulation and time to get back in touch with each other."[1]

More and more women in today's workforce are questioning the reasons they work outside the home. They are working smarter and, thus, learning to accomplish more in a shorter period of time. They are simplifying their lives, selling the mansions with the unmanageable mortgages, driving less expensive cars for longer periods of time, shopping less for clothes, living with fewer luxuries, and teaching their children to want less of society's cleverly advertised merchandise.

Smart women today are putting their priorities in order. They are spending more time with God in prayer, Bible study, devotional reading, family and congregational worship times. They are realizing their great need for personal Quiet time with God. They are allowing their tired bodies to seek silence and solitude. They are coming more often to the Quiet Place, and they are staying there longer.

Women today are questioning the things society holds so dear. They are figuring out what life's true values are. Many are choosing to retreat into simple lifestyles, those ways of living that leave them time for the things they truly treasure. They are turning their backs on the ideals promoted by retailers and Hollywood. They are yearning for a new simplicity, a "Walden Pond" type of life.

In 1845, Henry David Thoreau took inventory of his life and decided to turn his back on the hustle and bustle of Concord, Massachusetts. He built a simple cabin in the woods near Walden Pond, and in his book *Walden*, he records his eye-opening experiences of solitude and silence, urging his readers to simplify their lives. He writes,

> I went to the woods because I wished to live deliberately, to confront only the essential facts of life, and see if I could not learn what it had to teach, and not, when I came to die, discover that I had not lived.
>
> I did not wish to live what was no life, living is so dear, nor did I wish to practice resignation, unless it was quite necessary. I wanted to live deep and suck out all the marrow of life, to live so sturdily and Spartan-like as to put to rout all that was not life.[2]

Thoreau lived near Walden Pond for two years, two months, and two days, concentrating on what he called the essential facts of life. At the end of his sojourn there, with sensitive insight he asks, "Why should we live with such hurry and waste of life?"[3]

That is the question I have repeatedly asked myself for many years.

Think Through Your Priorities

As you think through your priorities, be sure to put solitude and silence at the top of your list.

- Make an appointment with God just as you would make appointments with clients and friends. Set aside certain times in your busy schedule to meet with your Father in heaven, to rest in His comfort, and to gain from His advice.

- Maintain some regularity in your daily schedule, not to the point of monotony or boredom, but to help you organize your day and prioritize your workload.

Contrary to Oswald Chambers, I believe it is important to establish a consistent daily routine. Chambers considered consistency "the hobgoblin of little minds," and to him, the "so-called practical side of life had little attraction."[4] However, for hardworking women, an *established* daily routine—rather than an *inflexible* one—helps to keep life more organized and the workload more evenly distributed. (That said, I do believe women should retreat from the routine on occasion to keep life from becoming dull and boring.)

Emilie Barnes writes,

> I've come to realize that all people need to get away from everything and everybody on a regular basis for thought, prayers, and just rest. For me this includes both daily quiet times and more extended periods of relaxation and replenishment. And it includes both times spent with my husband and periods of true solitude, spent with just me and God. These times of stillness offer me the chance to look within and nurture the real me. They keep me from becoming frazzled and depleted by the world around me.[5]

- Set aside time and space in your daily schedule to be still and to be with God. Allow yourself to "experience the fragrance of his love and let that love permeate [your] life, to let the calmness of His Spirit replenish the empty well of [your] heart, which gets depleted in the busyness and rush of the everyday demands and pressures."[6]

- Make your heart into a "quiet cell" where God can live and go with you during your day. Your time with God should not drain you but refresh you. Keep quiet time with Him simple and regular:

> The more we train ourselves to spend time with God and him alone, the more we will discover that God is with us at all times and in all places. Then we will be able to recognize Him even in the midst of a busy and active life.[7]

When we create simple and regular times and spaces to meet with God, we learn something important about ourselves, the way we work, and the way we try to please other people. We recognize our tendency to say yes to the requests others make of us and of our time. I like to say yes. I enjoy helping people who ask for my time and head and hands and legs. But, if we are to create ample space for our appointments with God in the Quiet Place, we must rethink our *automatic* yes response.

- Be honest with people who request your time. Don't say yes just to please them. Evaluate those reasons why you so naturally respond with a yes when it would be best for your workload and family to say no.
- Find a graceful way to say no when you choose to decline a request.

My friend Gracie loves her sister and her sister's school-aged boys, and she offered to help with the children. But Gracie discovered that her sister often requested more help than Gracie could give. Gracie decided to continue to help with the children but to spend less time with them. When her sister called, Gracie gently told her: "Sis, I love your kids! I enjoy being with them and caring for them. But I am spending so much time with them these days that my own work is suffering. I can't keep them this Saturday afternoon, but I'll look forward to seeing them some time after the weekend." Not only did Gracie's sister understand, she respected Gracie more for her honesty. Now when she asks for Gracie's help, she can depend on Gracie to be honest with her about her own work and time needs.

• Question the time-consuming, energy-draining things you do and why you do them. Select and delete those things that hold little value to you or anyone else.

I used to dread Christmas holidays for three primary reasons: (1) the exhausting parties I felt I needed to give and attend; (2) the shopping, traffic, and wrapping necessary for exchanging gifts with family and friends; and (3) the huge amount of time and money I spent to decorate and un-decorate the house for the holidays.

Christmas Parties

If a person invited me to a Christmas party, I used to believe I had to accept their invitation. I appreciated the kindness and hospitality extended to us by family and friends—I know the work involved in giving a party. But long before Thanksgiving our mailbox would overflow with party invitations. Most related to my husband's position as a seminary professor and later as a divinity school dean. Trying to attend numerous parties, we found ourselves tired, easily irritated, and complaining about lack of personal and family time. When our children were tiny, we spent more money than we had to spend on baby-sitters so that we could attend the parties and not disappoint anyone. By New Year's Day, my husband and I would collapse from exhaustion. Physically drained, we then jumped back into a full work schedule, having had no time to rest or enjoy the season. That's when we decided to take a long, hard look at Christmas.

"Why are we running back and forth to all these parties?" my husband asked. I had to admit, I didn't know.

"I guess I don't want to hurt people's feelings," I said. "People are kind to invite us. I feel like we're obligated to go."

"Do you really think they would miss us if we declined the invitation?" Timothy asked. I had to admit, as I thought back over numerous Christmas parties with crowds of people, that we probably wouldn't be missed if we didn't go. Now we rarely attend a Christmas party during the holidays. And when we do accept a party invitation, we are careful to look at our work and family schedule before we say yes.

Christmas Gifts

Not only did parties and get-togethers consume our holiday time but so did shopping and gift-buying. With every Christmas, gifts to and from family and friends became more numerous and more expensive. The fact was, nobody really needed anything! I spent tiring days in crowded shopping malls, waited literally hours in cashier's lines and traffic jams, and emptied our limited savings account. Often the gifts we gave (and received) ended up in overstuffed closets and garages; they were either the wrong size or color or people had no conceivable use for them.

I remember well the Christmas my mom and dad rented a U-Haul truck to bring our gifts to us on Christmas Eve! While we appreciated the thoughtfulness of our family and friends, as well as the gifts they bought, wrapped, and gave to us, things were getting out of hand.

One Sunday afternoon we sat down with our young children and had a serious talk about Christmas gift-giving. Fortunately, our pastor, Dr. Charles Carter, had preached a sermon that morning at church on missionaries and how they needed our money to support their work. My eight-year-old daughter, Alyce, had taken Dr. Carter's words to her little heart. Alyce listened intently while we talked and then offered this suggestion:

"I got an idea!" she exclaimed. "Why don't we take the money we usually spend on Christmas presents and give it to the missionaries?"

My ten-year-old son, Christian, didn't think that was such a great plan. "What?!" he interrupted. "Not get Christmas presents at Christmas?!"

Soon, however, Christian agreed with the rest of us: We decided as a family to forego gift-giving that Christmas. We took pencil and paper, and we figured up the amount of money we usually spent for gifts. Then we wrote a check for Dr. Carter to send to the missionaries. When we told our family and friends, they liked the idea. I think I might have even heard a small sigh of relief.

Was Christmas that year meaningful? Yes! It was one of the most memorable holidays we have ever had. Without shopping, fighting traffic, hunting for parking places, standing in long lines at stores and post offices, and wrapping gifts past midnight, we enjoyed a peaceful, restful, and much more worshipful season.

Just think of how many things you and I do—each day, each week, each month, and each year—that we could easily stop doing and no one would even notice, much less care. I must admit to you, since I filled out my "priority list," I am doing much less housework, having fewer dinner parties, folding fewer towels (why do we fold towels?), ironing fewer clothes, and going to fewer get-togethers. No, I don't have the most perfectly kept house. You certainly can't eat off my floor. And my house wouldn't pass the white-glove test. But who cares? I do what I can and let the rest of it go. It has freed me up for more important things, like personal Bible study and prayer time, solitude, and time spent with my husband, children, extended family, and friends.

Christmas Decorations

While our neighbors are clinging to ladders, dangling from rooftops, and replacing twinkling light bulbs in their bushes, we are gathered around a fireplace, watching old movies, and eating popcorn. When I tell people (only those who ask!) that we no longer decorate for Christmas, they smile and call me "Scrooge." While they are trying to rearrange heavy family room furniture to make space for an eight-foot tree, untangling last year's lights, and cleaning up broken glass ornaments, we are enjoying quiet time both individually and together. Some Christmases we have chosen to put up a few decorations. But we keep them simple. And we enjoy the decorations of those people who enjoy decorating for Christmas.

- Think through family holiday traditions. Throw out those that hold little meaning to you or your family. Keep those traditions that are meaningful and a vital part of your holiday fun.
- Strive to concentrate more on the reason for the season (Thanksgiving, birthdays, Christmas, Easter, anniversaries, etc.) and less on the time-consuming trimmings.
- Travel during the holidays only when you must! After spending a few Christmas Days stranded in the nation's crowded airports, we try to stay home during the busy holidays.
- Stop "going with the flow" and think seriously about why you do what you do. Save your physical energy for things that hold ultimate meaning to you and your family.

If you need help considering your life's priorities, make a list like the one below. It can show you on paper the things you value and don't value, as well as the work that is necessary for you to do and the things you can leave undone. Make new priority lists as your life changes.

MY PRIORITY LIST

The three most important things in my life are:

1.

2.

3.

My family's most pressing needs right now are:

1.

2.

3.

The three things (or more) that must be done today, this week, this month are:

(Today)

1.

2.

3.

(This week)

1.

2.

3.

(This month)

1.

2.

3.

The three things (or more) today, this week, this month, that I can leave undone are:

(Today)

1.

2.

3.

(This week)

1.

2.

3.

(This month)

1.

2.

3.

The three things I'd like to do if time permits are:

1.

2.

3.

The three things that bring me tremendous joy, comfort, pleasure, and a sense of well-being are:

1.

2.

3.

Ways I can learn to live one day at a time, and to truly find God's peace and joy in the loveliness of the present moment, are:

1.

2.

3.

- Live each day deliberately, and be enjoyably present in the moment. Frederick C. Van Tatenhove writes,

    I am still learning to live today, today. Each day I try

to pause intentionally for a moment of rest and quiet enjoyment of something present. Many times it's to watch a sunrise through my living room window or to ponder quietly the blessings of my life or to marvel at the vastness of a starry summer night or to listen to the steady sound of a spring rain. These experiences help me to live in the present. They become moments of devotion that move me to worship God.[8]

SIMPLIFY AND DE-CLUTTER YOUR LIFE

- Get rid of those things in your home and office and car that you no longer use or need.
- Strive to de-clutter your surroundings. Make it a family work project. Give the items you no longer use, the clothes and shoes that no longer fit, to someone who needs them.
- Detach yourself from your possessions.
- Create open and uncluttered space in your environment.
- Always be ready to "uproot" if God calls you to a different place.

Oswald Chambers believed: "It is a great thing to be detached enough from possessions so as not to be held by them, because when called to uproot it is done with little real trouble."[9]

- Shop only when you must. If you presently visit shopping malls for recreation, find another place to go. Professional advertisers strive to lure us to buy stuff we don't really need. The temptation to spend money is just too great in some places.
- Be content with what you possess, and stop striving to collect more clutter. Leith Anderson, in his book *Becoming Friends With God*, exposes the potential pride and possessiveness caused by ownership:

We like to defend our territory. Whenever we can

wedge in a word, we like to brag about our house, our car, the office where we work, our salary, or our net worth. Frankly, many of us hold so tightly to what we have that our knuckles are white and our lives are stressed with possessiveness and fear.[10]

- Give away as much money as you can. Generously support missionaries, constructive church programs, worthwhile community projects, etc. Master money. Never allow money to master you.
- View money not as a prized possession but as a necessary tool. Says J. C. Ryle,

> Money is one of the most unsatisfying of possessions. It takes away some cares, no doubt; but it brings with it quite as many cares as it takes away. There is the trouble in the getting of it. There is anxiety in the keeping of it. There are temptations in the use of it. There is guilt in the abuse of it. There is sorrow in the losing of it. There is perplexity in the disposing of it.[11]

- Learn to be content with what you have.

> One of the most pervasive and destructive mental tendencies I've seen is that of focusing on *what we want instead of what we have*. It doesn't seem to make any difference how much we have; we just keep expanding our list of desires, which guarantees we will remain dissatisfied. The mind-set that says "I'll be happy when this desire is fulfilled" is the same mind-set that will repeat itself once that desire is met.[12]

The apostle Paul writes, "I have learned to be content whatever the circumstances. I know what it is to be in need, and I know what it is to have plenty. I have learned the secret of being content in any and every situation" (Philippians 4:11–12). The writer of Hebrews tells us to "keep your lives free from the love of money and be content with what you have" (13:5).

- Be wise about retirement: Invest wisely, save some money, and plan your financial future, but don't obsessively spend your life laboring in stress and fear. In his book *The Hand of God*, Alistair Begg asks an interesting question and gives me much food for thought:

    Are we going to buy into the mythology that we need to kill ourselves trying to "make it" for as many years as we can so that we can line the nest in which we plan to hibernate? If we believe this, our whole lives will become merely preparation for hibernation.[13]

TAKE CARE OF YOUR BODY

- Treat your physical body as you would care for a precious gift. God created for you this miracle. Be grateful to Him, and be good to it, and it will serve Him and you well.
- Eat healthy. Eat only the amount of food your body needs.
- If you need to lose weight, talk with your doctor and shed those unwanted pounds.
- Rest your body often. Get the amount of sleep that your body needs.
- Don't expose your body to unnecessary danger. Are you one of America's hardcore thrill seekers? If you are, find something else! It's not worth the health risk and potential permanent injury.
- Protect your body. Dress it appropriately for the weather. Buckle it into the car seat. Don't take unnecessary risks with it.
- Keep your body clean. Protect it from unnecessary germs.
- Please don't smoke!

I feel especially strong in giving this last bit of advice. My own dad lost a lung to tobacco use, and eventually smoking-related diseases took his life. He started smoking as a teenager, in those days when it was considered cool. Today we know that smoking is not cool. It is deadly to the human body. Let me share with you some medical facts about smoking:

Did you know that about forty-eight million adults in the U.S. smoke? More than three thousand teenagers start smoking each day. Smoking causes serious medical conditions, costing the nation $50 billion each year. Smoking causes one in five deaths, now killing nearly half a million people each year. About ten million people in the U.S. have died from smoking-related illnesses since 1964.

Smoking poses special risks for women. Female smokers have an increased risk of developing osteoporosis, having a miscarriage during pregnancy, and birthing a stillborn or low-birth-weight baby. Female smokers over age thirty-five who use birth-control pills are at high risk for heart attack, stroke, and blood clots in the legs.[14]

- Don't breathe someone else's cigarette smoke.

Not only is smoking deadly for the smoker, it also causes life-threatening health hazards to those who must breathe it.

Billions of people around the world who are exposed to secondhand smoke may have an increased risk of developing lung cancer. . . . Recent medical studies . . . showed passive smoking causes cancer . . . of the stomach, liver, kidneys, uterine cervix, and myeloid leukemia. "Involuntary smoking—breathing in secondhand smoke—is carcinogenic to humans," said Professor Jonathan Samet of Johns Hopkins University in Baltimore. . . . Tobacco smoke contains over 4,000 chemicals in the form of particles and gases. Carbon monoxide, ammonia, formaldehyde and hydrogen cyanide are among the potentially toxic ones. . . . People are harmed and killed by it.[15]

Even America's courts are taking secondhand-smoke health

issues more seriously. Recently a Miami jury "awarded $5.5 million in compensatory damages to Lynn French, 56, a flight attendant who does not smoke but has chronic sinus problems from spending more than a dozen years in smoky airplane cabins."[16]

- Listen to your body when it tells you it is overstressed or tired or needs to rest. We have already discussed how exhaustion and dis-stress can harm your health. When we don't protect our bodies, they will signal us with pain. That's how our body gets our undivided attention.

  "Sometimes our bodies will tell us a truth that our minds don't," writes Susan Forward. "We may say we're really not anxious—then notice that we're drenched with perspiration. No, no, nothing's wrong—so why is my stomach in knots? The body's responses cut through denial and rationalization, and the body won't lie to you."[17]

- Heed your body's warning signs and take them seriously.
- Research leading health hazards and diseases and learn how they can affect you.
- Take responsibility for your own physical health. Be consistent in your medical checkups. Pay attention to pain and other physical health warnings. Be aware of the latest health trends, warnings, and reports.

For instance, breast cancer awareness has received plenty of public attention in our nation recently. But did you know that heart disease is more dangerous? Heart disease kills many more women than breast cancer.

  Scientists have long known that cardiovascular disease hits women hard. The American Heart Association estimates that 240,000 women die from heart disease each year, making it the No. 1 killer of women over age 35 in the United States. Heart disease kills five times as many women as breast cancer.[18]

- Learn what you can do to prevent diseases that can hurt and even kill you. (For instance, did you know that exercise not only helps to relieve stress but also helps prevent stress-related diseases, such as heart disease in women?)

"Keeping heart attacks at bay doesn't have to mean hours of pumping iron and sweating it out on a health-club stair machine," a new study suggests. "For women, avoiding heart disease could be as easy as walking for 30 minutes a day." Dr. JoAnn Manson, professor of medicine at Harvard Medical School, states in the *New England Journal of Medicine* that this is "the first large-scale study in women to provide hard evidence that walking can significantly reduce the risk of heart attacks in women and that walking is sufficient to significantly impact that risk."[19]

TEACH YOUR DAUGHTERS AND SONS TO DEAL WITH STRESS

Stress more rapidly enters the lifestyles of our children today. If we are to prevent our children from suffering the effects of stress-related illnesses, we must teach them at an early age how to deal with stress. We must also manage our own stress because *our* stress will cause *them* stress.

Mary Minner, school counselor at Rosemary Hills Primary School in Silver Spring, Maryland, developed an eight-week stress management course for second graders. The goal? To help them "find that quiet on the inside," Ms. Minner said.

In a world where inner quiet is all too rare, much has been written about children and stress, especially since the terrorist attacks of September 11, 2001. Most books helped children overcome trauma such as divorce, serious illness, or the death of a loved one. Far less attention has been paid to helping young people cope with day-to-day stresses like taking tests, competing in sports, being invited to the right birthday parties and staving off playground bullies.

"Childhood is more stressful than ever," said Dr. Georgia Witkin, director of the Stress Program at the Mount Sinai School of Medicine in Manhattan, and author of *KidStress*.

"The best predictor of how a child will cope with stress is how the parent copes," says Dr. Edward Christophersen, of Children's Mercy Hospital in Kansas City, Missouri. "If a stressed mother slams the door and throws down her keys, she is teaching her child one way to relieve stress."

Dr. Witkin admits that there is no way to measure the extent of childhood stress, and health officials don't gather "kidstress" statistics. But she sees certain indicators in today's children.

"The Centers for Disease Control and Prevention reports that in 1997 a startling 21 percent of high school students had contemplated suicide in the previous year and that 8 percent had tried to kill themselves."[20]

DEAL WITH THE DIS-STRESS IN YOUR OWN LIFE

We already know that too much stress can be hazardous to our health. I recently read an eye-opening article about the effects stress can have on living creatures.

Biologist Kelly Zamudio, of Cornell University, made a disturbing discovery recently as he studied spotted salamanders throughout Canada and the United States. Salamanders across the continent had spots similar in size; the spots matched up one for one on the left and right sides of their backs.

When he compared these healthy salamanders with salamanders he found at various golf courses around the country, he discovered that the animals living at golf courses had irregular spots. Some of the spots were different sizes, or there were more spots on one side of the animal than on the other side. After careful analysis, Zamudio pointed out that the salamanders with irregular spots were victims of "population stress."

A stressed-out salamander?

Zamudio explains,

Abnormal spots don't necessarily mean an animal is unhealthy. But it does indicate that there's something in the environment that's causing a disruption in some developmental stage. . . . Changing spots can act as an early warning system, both for the salamander and other animals.

Something is happening to them. This might be a great tool for trying to figure out which populations of amphibians are stressed before they actually go extinct.[21]

Now comes the obvious question: If everyday environmental stress can cause a healthy salamander to change its spots, just imagine what environmental stress can do to the body of today's woman! Surely it might be a good idea "to figure out which populations [of women] are stressed before they actually go extinct"!

- Strive to eliminate unnecessary stress from your daily life.
- Learn to recognize stress and its symptoms. Figure out what is causing it.

Name your stress. The threat value of stress is reduced if you can move from a vague feeling of irritability, fatigue, or being overwhelmed by pressure to a focus on the source of the stress. It may be due to factors in your physical environment, family relationships, work situation, health, or other personal concerns.[22]

- Create spaces of time between stressful events.

You do not have full control of all the stress events that occur in your life. You do have control over some of the stresses that happen to you. You can spread some of them out by putting more time between the stressful events.[23]

How can we do this?

Deferring the time of a job change, a wedding, a

change in residence, a mortgage, a change in church activities, very often is within the range of your control. Spread such events out over a period of time. Create some lapses of time between stress events as much as possible. This will bring a measure of serenity and help you manage the stress more effectively.[24]

Calm the "Hurry" Rhythm of Your Body

- Slow down. Stop hurrying through life.
- Don't over-commit yourself.
- Have some fun!
- Enjoy life's roses!

As we strive to work through our lengthy To-Do lists, we fall into health-harming habits. One of these is the habit of hurry. Not only do we hurry through work, we hurry through play, family get-togethers, and personal time with God.

"So many of us live our lives as if the secret purpose is to somehow get everything done. We stay up late, get up early, [and] avoid having fun."[25]

Is finishing everything on the day's To-Do list really so important that in the meantime we miss out on life?

Why do we hurry ourselves like we do? We don't stop to smell the roses. In fact, we hardly see the roses!

"Hurrying becomes a habit," writes Elaine St. James. "Even after we've simplified many of our daily routines, if we're still surrounded by fast-moving people and phones that never stop ringing, slowing down can take a major effort."[26]

Even worse than pushing our own bodies like they are lifetime-guaranteed machines, we sometimes push our children. We hurry them not only throughout the day but also from event to event throughout the years.

In *The Hurried Child*, child psychologist David Elkind reports that he "no longer sees spoiled children, but children who are thrust into adult roles too soon. . . . Hurried children grow up too fast, pushed in their early years toward many different types of achievement and exposed to experiences that tax their adaptive capacity."[27]

Surely it's no wonder that "stress-related problems, usually confined to adults, are developing in children at earlier ages." Why? Because when "faced with adult tasks and tensions before they are prepared emotionally and psychologically, children feel bewildered and stressed."[28]

- Take regular vacations and create quiet times both for yourself and your children.
- Take time off from work and do nothing but rest.
- Seek quiet places to retreat. Create quiet places for your kids to retreat.
- Allow God to envelope you in His presence and eagerly receive His life-sustaining blessings.

When Marilyn Chandler McEntyre took time away from her busy schedule and went away for a spiritual retreat, she found the rhythm of her life changing for the better.

"About the third day I began really to be there, to receive the blessing of quiet time, reflection, prayer, worship, and unhurried conversation about things that matter," she remembers. "My sense of spiritual refreshment was palpable by the end of the week. I breathed differently. I did not wake up with morning headaches. I walked in a keener awareness of God's enveloping presence."

In reflecting on her experience of quiet and rest, McEntyre surmises, "I'd like life to be a series of pauses like a poem, rather than a fast-paced, page-turner airport novel."

The culture teaches us that "downtime" is wasted. Time is money. . . . As the tempo of cultural life speeds up, the heartbeat of daily life races, *and our own body rhythms respond with adrenaline, cramped muscles, and heart attacks.* To take time daily for prayer, for a quiet walk that's not to the next meeting, for daydreaming or for an unplanned conversation is a countercultural act.[29]

CREATE A SUPPORT GROUP OF FRIENDS

I don't know what I would do if I had to live without my friends! You can trust good friends, and good friends can nurture and support you physically, mentally, emotionally, and spiritually.

- Surround yourself with trusted, loving friends.
- Choose friends who share your Christian beliefs, and spend time with them in prayer and fellowship.
- Nurture your friends, and allow your friends to nurture you.
- "Tend" and "befriend" those who deal with heavy workloads and tiring schedules.

Did you know that women react to stress differently than men do? Women tend to turn to friends when they are dis-stressed or feel tense. Men show a stronger fight-or-flight reflex than most women do. When women have a bad day at the office, for example, they tend to respond by caring for their children or getting together with friends. Women need friends to help relieve everyday stress.

SURROUND YOURSELF WITH SILENCE AND SOLITUDE

- Become consciously aware of the noise level in your home or workplace. Protect yourself from external racket and loud noises. Learn to create quiet.

Start becoming aware of the continuously high noise levels you are subjected to every day. It often begins with the nerve-jangling clamor of the alarm clock, the buzz of an electric toothbrush, or the blast of a hair dryer. This is followed by the drone of the latest news report or the babble of morning talk shows. Then comes the revving of car engines, and the honking of horns in rush hour traffic. Our days are often filled with the nine-to-five sounds of ringing telephones and office equipment, not to mention the countless interruptions of coworkers, customers, and bosses.[30]

CONSIDER BUYING A FISHING POLE AND LEARNING HOW TO FISH!

In spite of getting worm-dirt under your fingernails or getting "finned" by a fish or hooking your hand, I have discovered that fishing invites me to silence and solitude. All avid, passionate fisherpeople know there's much more to fishing than just catching something.

TAKE THE STRESS TEST!

To measure the amount of stress you are currently experiencing, see the Holmes/Masuda Social Readjustment Rating Scale below. Check those stressors you have faced within the past year. Give yourself the experience's point value. Then add together the points to find out your own level of stress. Remember, if at any given time your total points add up to three hundred or more, you should stop and take note, for, according to Holmes and Masuda, you are overstressed and in danger of becoming sick.

Social Readjustment Rating Scale
(Holmes and Masuda)

100 points—Death of spouse
73 points—Divorce
65 points—Marital separation
63 points—Jail term
63 points—Death of close family member
53 points—Personal injury or illness
50 points—Marriage

47 points—Fired at work

45 points—Marital reconciliation

45 points—Retirement

44 points—Change in health of family member

40 points—Pregnancy

39 points—Sex difficulties

39 points—Gain of new family member

39 points—Business readjustment

38 points—Change in financial state

37 points—Death of close friend

36 points—Change to different line of work

35 points—Change in number of arguments with spouse

31 points—Mortgage over $10,000

30 points—Foreclosure of mortgage or loan

29 points—Change in responsibilities at work

29 points—Son or daughter leaving home

29 points—Trouble with in-laws

28 points—Outstanding personal achievement

26 points—Spouse begins or stops work

26 points—Begin or end school

25 points—Change in living conditions

24 points—Revision of personal habits

23 points—Trouble with boss

20 points—Change in work hours or conditions

20 points—Change in residence

20 points—Change in schools

19 points—Change in recreation

19 points—Change in church activity

18 points—Change in social activities

17 points—Mortgage or loan less than $10,000

16 points—Change in sleeping habits

15 points—Change in number of family get-togethers

15 points—Change in eating habits
13 points—Vacation
12 points—Christmas
11 points—Minor violations of the law*[31]

---

*Notes to reader: (1) Holmes and Masuda compiled this scale when home mortgages were much less than they are today; (2) This scale also helps us to understand the level of stress a family member or friend may be experiencing.

Chapter Eleven

TRANSFORMING OUR BODY

M an cannot long survive without air, water, and sleep. Next in importance comes food. And close on its heels, solitude."[1]

Seek solitude and silence. Treasure them. Protect them. Our times of solitude and silence help replenish our tired bodies, relieve our everyday stress, give us time to breathe deeply, to think, to ponder life, and to rest our souls. Silence and solitude can energize us so that we can return to our workloads with greater physical strength and endurance. They also help us decide which workloads are worth returning to—which *majors* to keep and which *minors* to discard.

Scripture tells us our physical body is a temple of God's Holy Spirit. God designed our bodies to function well and to serve Him, others, and ourselves. Let us accept His gift of a physical body with gratefulness. Let us doubly thank Him if our bodies are strong and healthy. The human body is a miracle! Let us take good care of it.

Be altruistic but take care of yourself at the same time.
If you are going to serve others well, you must at the same

time survive and do well yourself.

Let us consider Nature's model as we think about our bodies. All the tissues in your body are altruistic except cancer cells. Cooperate with your own tissues. The *joie de vivre,* or joy of life, has an enormous preventive and healing effect.[2]

THE VALUE OF PHYSICAL REST

Rest your body. It needs the tender loving care that rest brings to it. Human bodies aren't machines. They cannot work and produce without regular periods of total rest. They require time to replenish themselves. God created our body to need physical rest.

Scripture tells us that even God himself rested on the seventh day of Creation. He wasn't tired, but still He rested. In six days He created the universe and everything in it, including our ancestors, Adam and Eve. But on the seventh day, God stopped His work and He rested. Scripture tells us:

> By the seventh day God had finished the work he had been doing; so on the seventh day he rested from all his work. And God blessed the seventh day and made it holy, because on it he rested from all the work of creating that he had done. (Genesis 2:2–3)

In His Word, God encourages us to follow His example to rest:

> There remains, then, a Sabbath-rest for the people of God; for anyone who enters God's rest also rests from his own work, just as God did from his. Let us, therefore, make every effort to enter that rest. (Hebrews 4:9–11)

No doubt God knew we would allow hard work to overwhelm our fragile bodies. So He specified one day of the week and blessed it for the purpose of physical rest.

The writer of Hebrews uses the Greek word *sabbatismos* in this passage. *Sabbatismos* means "a rest from all work, a rest like that of God when He had finished the work of creation."[3]

Jesus uses a different word in Matthew 11:28, when He offers us His rest: "Come to Me, all you who labor. . . . And I will give you *rest*" (NKJV, emphasis mine). The Greek word Jesus uses is *anapausis,* and it means a "rest from weariness."[4]

Without adequate rest, we will quickly deplete our energy resources and become physically exhausted. When that happens, we suffer, our family suffers, and our work suffers.

JESUS RESTED

Jesus took time away from work and others—times of solitude—in order to physically rest. Certain days in His public ministry Jesus and His disciples worked so hard that they had no chance to eat. One day, "because so many people were coming and going that [Jesus and the disciples] did not even have a chance to eat, [Jesus] said to them, 'come with me by yourselves to a quiet place and get some rest' " (Mark 6:31). They then "went away by themselves in a boat to a solitary place" (6:32).

"Come with me by yourselves"—*solitude*—"to a quiet place"—*silence*—"and get some rest," Jesus said. Jesus includes solitude, silence, and rest in His command, for He knows tired, overworked bodies need all three elements to replenish themselves.

Mark writes of another time when Jesus was physically exhausted and needed to rest from weariness. Jesus and His disciples stepped into a boat and pushed it out onto Lake Galilee. After he curled up to sleep in the boat's stern, His body was so tired that even when a "furious squall" blew in, and the "waves broke over the boat, so that it was nearly swamped," Jesus didn't wake up.

The frightened disciples, fearing for their lives, woke Him. Jesus got up, "rebuked the wind and said to the waves, 'Quiet!

Be still!' " The wind and waves obeyed, and "it was completely calm" (see Mark 4:35–41).

Jesus knew when to rest His tired body, and He leaves us a wonderful example of the importance of physical rest. He gives you and me permission, in His Word and through His own example, to stop our work, to lie down, and to rest when our bodies are tired. We must never *feel guilty* when we need to lie down and rest. God has given us the wonderful gifts of rest and sleep to renew our depleted strength.

Elijah Rested

Proper rest will transform our physical bodies. When the Old Testament prophet Elijah grew weary, God made him rest. Elijah had an exciting victory on Mount Carmel (see 1 Kings 19), and that show of spiritual strength together with God's power made Jezebel a very unhappy queen. Wicked to the core, Jezebel threatened to kill Elijah, sending her troops out to find and destroy him.

Elijah was overcome with fear and fled for his life. He ran more than one hundred miles, then walked for another whole day deep into the wilderness. To trek that great distance, we must assume Elijah was a healthy man, with strong, muscular legs. But Elijah was weary. His recent experience with wet bulls and Baal's prophets at Mount Carmel had exhausted him. His legs hurt from running. He finally stopped his flight and sat down under a tree. He had had enough.

Have you ever felt like that? Have you ever sat down, feeling defeated, head in your hands, and admitted: "I've had enough"?

I have. Many times. I have discovered that times like these are not good times to make life-changing decisions. Rather, they are times to rest and pray. Times to put my tired head on God's gracious shoulder and rest—to find *anapausis*—from my weariness.

Let's visit Elijah as he sits under the broom tree, defeated in spirit, weary in body: "I have had enough, Lord," Elijah says. He asks God to let him die (1 Kings 19:4). Listen to God's response. Does God give Elijah a lecture on running away from responsibility? No. Does God scold Elijah for his lack of trust in the Lord, his Protector? No. Does God grant Elijah's wish and allow him to die? No.

God knows exactly what Elijah needs as he sits tired and depressed under the *broom tree*! A broom tree is a large bush that grows in the Dead Sea wilderness area. Its large bushy branches span out to form an umbrella of shade, and its foliage and roots were often burned and used as fuel in ancient times (see Psalm 120:4). Ancient people ate the roots for food (see Job 30:4); the broom tree also produces beautiful white flowers with deep-maroon centers.

We must not let the significance of the broom tree escape us in our quick reading of this passage. The symbolism of this wilderness plant is as beautiful as the One who created it and places the weary Elijah beneath it.

- The broom tree spreads its branches over Elijah and shades him—protects him—from the blazing Middle-Eastern sun. Elijah needs comfort and protection in his exhausted state. In Elijah's Quiet Place, as in our own Quiet Places, God spreads His arms around us—loving, comforting, and protecting us.

- The broom tree provides fuel and food to anyone who sits beneath it. In this Quiet Place, Elijah is given the necessary resources to build a fire (fuel) as well as the life-sustaining food to cook over the fire. In our own Quiet Places, God provides physical renewal (spiritual *fuel*) and strengthening sustenance (spiritual *food*)—all the necessary resources to get us back on our feet.

- The broom tree, with its desert flowers of maroon and white, offers Elijah the beauty he needs to recall his gratefulness to God. The flowers are his icing on the cake, so to speak. Only a loving Father gives His children so much more than their basic needs.[5]

Protection and shade, fuel and food, flowers and beauty are not the only sources of renewal and rest that God gives Elijah. God also sends an angel—His own personal messenger—to Elijah. The angel carries a cake of bread and a jar of water, touching Elijah and saying, "Get up and eat." Elijah eats the bread and drinks the water, and then he lies down and sleeps. Later the angel comes back to check on him. "Get up and eat, Elijah," the angel tells him. Elijah eats again, and the food, water, and physical rest strengthen him. Replenished and physically renewed, Elijah climbs to his feet and travels for the next forty days and nights until he reaches Mount Horeb.

Elijah doesn't need a lecture. Elijah needs physical sustenance. He needs food, water, and rest. Just like you do. Just like I do.

Dr. Wayne Oates once told me, "Denise, when you counsel with a couple who is considering divorce, the first question you should ask them is this: 'How much sleep do you both get at night?' " Dr. Oates said that he believed most divorces are caused by a husband and wife's lack of sleep and adequate rest.

Think about your own life, your marriage, your physical needs, and your state of exhaustion and unrest. How much sleep do you get at night? Adequate sleep, and time spent with God in the Quiet Place, will refresh you like God-refreshed (and revived) Elijah under the gracious broom tree.

Sometimes women see the need to rest their bodies as a kind of failure. They may even feel guilty when they admit their exhaustion and stop to rest.

Says Jill Briscoe,

> The good news is . . . [God] waits around the corner . . . with the teapot boiling, the bread hot upon the stones, and our bed ready with turned down covers! He has a plan—a plan of renewal and refreshment—and he waits at the reception desk of Broom Tree Inn, ready and eager to check us in! What we need to do is cooper-

ate. We should lie down and sleep. We should get up and eat. Then we should lie down and sleep again![6]

"Come to Me," Jesus calls to us, "*all you who labor* . . . and I will give you rest." Let's take Jesus up on His offer!

Section Three
SPIRIT REST

Laden

JESUS SAID:
"COME TO ME, ALL YOU WHO ARE HEAVY
LADEN AND I WILL GIVE YOU REST."
(MATTHEW 11:28 NKJV)

Chapter Twelve

YOKED WITH HEAVY BURDENS

Jesus invites all of us who are "heavy ladened" or "*soul* burdened" or "*heart* burdened" to come to Him. *Soul* (or *spirit*) "is a cipher for our spiritual attributes, like being courageous or timid. *Heart* is the most important term in [Scripture] for referring to the inner nature." For instance, Jesus tells us to "love the Lord your God with all your *heart*" (Matthew 22:37). This means "we are to love God with every fiber of our being."[1]

I am discovering that, in some ways, all women are "heavy ladened" and somewhat "soul-burdened." Some of us wear heavy yokes placed on us by other people, people who have unrealistic expectations for us, people who expect *us* to handle *their* emergencies, people who believe we must do *their* work. Others of us wear heavy yokes placed on us by society, bosses, co-workers, in-laws, and even circumstances. Some of us wear heavy yokes that we, for whatever reason, place on our own necks.

Maybe you carry in your heart a heavy burden. Perhaps your soul is heavy laden and weary. If so, I have an answer for you, no matter how heavy your burden, no matter how ladened your soul. His name is Jesus. He loves you perfectly. And He waits, right now, for you to join Him in the Quiet Place. There you can talk and cry and commune with Him in sacred solitude. There you can place your head on His strong shoulder and find rest for your heart and soul. You need no longer wear the heavy, burdensome yoke alone. Jesus invites you to take His yoke upon you and learn from Him. He promises that His yoke is easy to wear and His burden is light.

Jesus chose a perfect and beautiful example when He used the image of the yoke. In ancient days in the Middle East, Egypt, and other lands, a farmer chose two hardworking, muscular animals, usually oxen, to plow his fields. If you've ever walked through the Holy Land, you know the fields require strong beasts to pull the plows. The ground, sun-baked and hard as brick, is covered with large and small rocks.

Yokes were heavy wooden harnesses that kept two animals walking side by side. Placed upon the animals' necks, the yoke ensured that each ox pulled in relatively equal strength in order to plow the hard ground. They shared the heavy burden. As the animals struggled to pull the attached plow, the rough wood of the yoke scraped and tore at their shoulders and necks.

"The yokes used in the East are very heavy, and press so much upon the animals that they are unable to bend their necks."[2]

Ancient Middle-Eastern oxen knew all about carrying heavy burdens—it was their life work. Sometimes the farmer raised or bought an untrained plow animal. In order to teach the younger, weaker animal to wear the yoke and plow the field, the farmer yoked him to a muscular, experienced ox. The strong, well-trained ox bore the bulk of the yoke while the newer animal learned how to plow. While the yoke on the experienced animal proved doubly heavy, the animal trainee's yoke was light and easy.

When Jesus uses this yoke example, He offers us, the weaker trainee, to share the yoke with Him, the experienced muscular

One. We walk beside Him, work with Him, and learn from Him, but He takes the burdens and carries them for us. He pulls the plow. He offers us His divine rest from our heavy burdens (see Matthew 11:29–30 NKJV).

Matthew Henry calls the yoke Jesus offers us "a yoke . . . lined with love" and "a yoke of pleasantness." Henry said that we need not fear His yoke. "His commandments are holy, just, and good. It requires self-denial, and exposes us to difficulties, but this is abundantly repaid, even in this world, by inward peace and joy."[3]

It is in the Quiet Place that we hear Jesus' offer to carry our heart's burdens. It is in solitude and silence that we can offer Him our ladened soul and enter into rest. Why do you and I so often lug our heavy hearts and weary souls all by ourselves when Jesus waits to help us carry the bulk of the load?

> Jesus promises that his yoke will be kind and gentle to our shoulders, enabling us to carry our load more easily. That is what he means when he says his burden is "light." Actually, it might be quite heavy, but we will be able to carry it. Why? Because Jesus himself will help us. It is as though he tells us, "Walk alongside me; learn to carry the burden by observing how I do it. If you let me help you, the heavy labor will seem lighter."[4]

What burdens your heart today? What keeps your soul heavy laden? Is it fear? Or guilt? Or depression? Or worry? Or hate? Or bitterness? Or selfishness? Or deceit? Or pride? Or lust? Or sadness? Or despair?

The list could go on almost indefinitely. Women today, around the world, are burdened by many things. The more I travel, the more I realize that most of the problems women face are universal. As I've talked with women in Japan and England and Europe and the Middle East, as well as other places around the globe, I have been amazed to discover how closely their individual problems resemble the current struggles of American women. They too deal with such things as fear of job loss, heavy work stress, financial difficulties, marital conflict, divorce, abandonment, spousal abuse, parenting and grandparenting problems, deaths of loved ones, a loved one's suicide, personal illness, serious surgery, caring for ill or elderly parents, depression, natural disasters, war, terrorism; and the list goes on.

And the more deeply I study Scripture, the more convinced I am that these problems cross time barriers as well as geographic barriers. Women in Jesus' day, the first century, suffered many if not most of the same problems you and I deal with today in the twenty-first century! For instance, consider these biblical women and their problems:

- Abuse, abandonment, and racial prejudice: The Samaritan woman Jesus encountered at Jacob's Well.

This woman from Samaria knew intense hatred and discrimination because of her race. Samaritans took the brunt of abuse from those in society who called them "half-breeds." Not only did she deal with racial injustice but also with undependable husbands. John tells us that she'd had five husbands, who likely had abused and abandoned her. She now lived with a man who used her but hadn't married her.

The Samaritan woman's experience is similar to that of many American women today. Many women of color still deal with society's hatred and prejudice. They also cope with husbands who batter them, or abandon them, or divorce them. They too know daily abuse and marital conflict and racial slurs.

To abused women—of the twenty-first century as well as the first century—Jesus reaches out with understanding, freedom of soul, and eternal salvation (see John 4:1–42): "Come to Me," He calls. "I will give you rest" from your burdens.

- Fear and Guilt: The sinful woman.

Pulled away from an immoral sexual union, this frightened, naked woman was thrown down on the crowded temple court-yard to be sentenced to death. In those days, religious leaders rigidly followed the law of Moses regarding adultery: Death by stoning (although the man who was with her was not brought along). Panic and guilt enveloped her. When asked to intervene, to himself pronounce the execution, Jesus instead rescued the woman from her accusers and then forgave her wrongdoing and told her not to repeat her sin. He set her soul free from fear and guilt.

To frightened and guilt-burdened women today, like this woman, Jesus reaches out in tenderness and sets free the miserable soul (see John 8:1–11).

• Grief and Despair: Martha and Mary, who grieved the death of their brother, Lazarus.

Like women today, when Martha and Mary's brother, Lazarus, died, the sisters deeply mourned. They had lost a loved one to death, an inevitable occurrence in most women's lives. In deep despair, both sisters reached out to Jesus for comfort and encouragement.

Jesus approached Martha and Mary as individuals when He comforted them. Martha needed a theological explanation of death and resurrection and eternal life. So Jesus gave her a sermon, and it brought hope and joy to Martha even in the midst of her brother's death. Mary, on the other hand, needed someone to cry with her. She didn't want a sermon, she wanted someone to soothe her soul. Jesus simply wept with Mary, and His sacred tears dissolved her despair and gave her hope.

Women today also deeply grieve the death of loved ones. Their souls also experience the sadness and despair death brings. To grieving women today, as to Martha and Mary, Jesus reaches out with encouragement and comfort, with the good news of His resurrection. To us who grieve, Jesus calls, "Come to Me" and gives us a taste of Easter (see John 11:1–44).

- Sickness, Discrimination, and Handicap: The bleeding woman and the crippled woman.

This desperately sick woman had bled for a dozen years with no cure in sight. First-century Jews held that women during their menstrual periods were ceremonially unclean, in accordance with Levitical law. This poor woman was hemorrhaging! They made her shout, "Unclean! Unclean!" as she walked through the streets. Upon hearing her voice, the crowds parted to avoid touching her, for if they had contact with her, they too would be made "unclean." She suffered an embarrassing, devastating illness that isolated her from those she loved. One day, as Jesus walked through the crowds of people, she bravely reached out and touched His robe.

> The woman who reaches out and grabs the "hem of his garment" actually touched one of the 613 tassels hanging from Jesus' prayer shawl, or tallit, which Jesus wore whenever he went outside. Every shawl is embroidered with 613 tassels around the fringe—one tassel for each of the laws of the Torah. The point of these tassels is not to show off one's knowledge of the Torah. The purpose of these tassels is to symbolize that when one prays, one literally wraps oneself in the healing, life-giving Word of God. That is why when the woman who has been "unclean" for twelve years touches one of Jesus' tassels, Jesus does not recoil in horror but reaches down, holds, heals, and helps her to her feet.[5]

Immediately her bleeding stopped. Jesus healed this woman from an unclean disease.

He said to her, "*Daughter*, your faith has healed you. Go in peace and be freed from your suffering" (see Mark 5:25–34).

I wonder how long it had been since anyone called her "daughter"?

While the bleeding woman *touched Jesus*, the crippled woman in Luke 13 was *touched by Jesus* and made well. In those days, a sick or handicapped person was considered by society a "nonperson." Usually she was escorted out of the community and made to live a hermit's life. She had no social standing. Many people considered her to be less than human. The crippled woman not only suffered an isolating handicap but as an elderly woman she also coped with age discrimination. When she entered the temple to worship God, other worshipers would either show their contempt or completely ignore her. They either abused her or deemed her invisible.

But Jesus noticed her. He healed her of her handicap, and for the first time in eighteen years she stood up straight. Then Jesus rebuked the church leaders who had kept her in emotional isolation. He humiliated the self-righteous "sons of Abraham" in a way that caused them to lower their heads and slither away. He called her "a daughter of Abraham"! In other words, Jesus restored her place in God's family. He demonstrated her personhood, her self-esteem, her unique worth to society and the religious community. Nowhere in the entire Bible did anyone ever refer to a woman as "a daughter of Abraham." It remained a prestigious distinction held only for Jewish "sons of Abraham" (see Luke 13:10–17).

Age discrimination and disabilities and sickness plague women today as well. In fact, the American Association of Retired Persons (AARP) states that "age discrimination is now the fastest-growing type of complaint received by the Equal Employment Opportunity Commission. The second-fastest: discrimination based on disability."[6]

Some things never change—even after twenty centuries! Jesus, however, notices us when others don't. He names us His daughters, a definite and essential part of God's family. One touch and Jesus releases us from society's opinions. One touch and Jesus gives us new courage and new dignity and sets us back on our feet.

- Financial Stress, Worry, and Loss: The widow whose only son had died.

This widow deeply grieved her son's death. She cried with love for her lost son. But this woman had another reason to weep. In ancient days, a woman's financial support required a man: a father, a husband, or a son. Women without men were usually penniless. Decent employment for women was nonexistent. A poor woman without a financially supportive man was forced to become either a beggar or a prostitute.

Not only had this poor widow lost a much-loved son but she had also lost her bread and butter. She feared for her shelter—her life. Her financial security was gone.

Jesus knew her dilemma. He interrupted her son's funeral and whispered in her ear: "Don't cry." He ordered the dead son to get up and continue to support his mother! And he does. The funeral becomes a birthday! Jesus gave the boy back to his mother (see Luke 7:11–17).

Many women today also fear bleak or failing finances. On average, when a husband divorces his wife her income immediately decreases. Credit cards can also render consumers' heavy debt—offering the temptation of easy purchasing followed by high interest. Once women enter into debt, with borrowing rates as high as 21 percent, they find themselves struggling to free up their faltering financial futures. Advertisers spend billions of dollars luring potential consumers with delectable bait. Once hooked, a person can be caught in the deep waters of debt, distress, and even bankruptcy.

Americans today, especially older citizens, are incurring and paying off debt much later in their lives than even a few years ago. The percentage of older Americans debt-free in 1992 was 66 percent. Those older Americans debt-free in 2000 was only

41 percent.[7] As we have already seen, some women are now forced to forget about retirement and find new skills for new jobs in their later years.

Jesus shows a special tenderness for those women who live alone. He understands a single woman or widow's financial fears. He grieved the coming "widowing" of His own mother as He breathed His final breath. As Jesus died on the cross, He told His friend John to take care of His mother. From that time on Scripture says John took Mary into his home and loved her as his own mother (see John 19:26–27).

Jesus opens His arms to those who worry about life's basic needs—food and clothes—and says, "Don't worry about tomorrow—about your food or clothes, for your heavenly Father knows that you need them. Just come to Me . . . *trust Me, I am your provider* . . . bring Me your worries, your burdens. . . . I will give you rest" (see Matthew 6:25–34). "Here," He says, "slip this yoke over your shoulders. I'll bear the heavy burden for you; I'll take the weight of the yoke and pull the plow. Your part of the work will be light and easy. I can pull the load for both of us."

What are the emotional weights that burden our hearts and keep our souls from coming to the Quiet where God waits for us? Why do we choose to remain heavy laden with worries and concerns and frustrations and fears when Jesus offers us rest?

Chapter Thirteen

GUARDING OUR HEART

We cannot always control the things that happen to us: unexpected illnesses, deaths, or divorces that grip our heart and break it into small pieces. Pain caused by circumstances can leave us hurting. Suffering the offenses caused by others can drive our souls into deep despair. A woman can react in one of two ways when she faces suffering caused by circumstances or by those she has trusted: (1) She can allow the pain to draw her closer to God. She can answer His call, "Come to Me . . . and find rest." She can accept God's invitation to sit beneath His "broom tree" and be nurtured and renewed. Or (2) she can allow her suffering to make her bitter, to drive a wedge between herself and her heavenly Father. When she allows her sorrows to separate her from the One who truly loves her, the One who asks to wear her yoke, then she is doubly hurt. She causes herself even more pain, pain she doesn't need to suffer.

My sisters in Christ, let us guard our hearts against the potential enemy of *ourselves*. Let us stay alert and be careful what we allow to enter into our heart and our soul. Careless sins can separate us from God's gift of inner peace, tranquility, and rest. God doesn't stop loving us, or calling us to himself, but these enemies of the heart and soul can close our ears to His gentle whispers. They can cause us not to care anymore about our visits to the Quiet Place to spend time with Him. We stop missing Him, yearning for Him, and dreaming of Home. The tragedy caused by the enemy and the sins he invokes breaks down our communion with God. We must not allow this to happen. We must keep our heart and soul free from those things that will rob us of our intimate relationship with the Lord.

Many sin-separators threaten to destroy communion in the Quiet Place: worry, dishonesty, lying, stealing, adultery, unfaithfulness, envy, jealousy, gossip, pride, love of money, conceit, misdirected ambition, etc. The following sins, however, top the list and do the most damage. These four sins set our feet on the well-worn path of destruction and despair: hate, prejudice, bitterness, and selfishness. (The second two will be addressed in chapter 14.)

GUARD YOUR HEART AGAINST HATE

Whenever you face hate, combat it with love. Hate is a cancer that attacks our heart and eats our soul. Hate "cells" attach themselves to healthy "cells" and multiply. They quickly take over a person's life and render it useless for God's kingdom work. You and I need no explanation of hate. We see the destructive enemy each morning when we open the daily newspaper, each evening when we turn on the TV news. We see hate in road rage and murder and terrorism. The only antidote to hate is love— unconditional and illogical *love*.

What is love? American women, even devoted Christian women, are often confused about its real meaning. Movies, magazines, and society in general have taught us falsehoods. Hollywood's version of love has nothing to do with Scripture's version. What society believes is true love is true lust. The sweaty hands, the thumping heart, the butterfly stomach—those prove to be *awesome* (wonderful and terrible) feelings, but they are *feelings*, not *fact*. While lust feelings soon evaporate, genuine love grows deeper with each passing day.

Genuine love is not a *feeling* at all. Real love is something we *do*—love is also a verb. Feelings have little to do with the love Scripture so beautifully defines. Let's look more deeply at biblical love.

In the English language, we have one word for love, and it is *love*. We use the same word to describe our affection for our mother as for our enjoyment of strawberry ice cream. We *love* God, and we *love* our children. We *love* our country, and we *love* our country club. We *love* to fish, and we *love* to eat out with our spouse. Our one word *love* makes no distinction between degrees of affection or strength of conviction. The context of our statement must awkwardly hint at the type of love we mean.

Biblical Love Versus Societal Love

People in Jesus' day had several separate and distinctive words for "love." No one had to stop and guess what another meant when He used the most beautiful biblical word for love: *agape*. *Agape* is that perfect, selfless, unconditional, I-love-you-no-matter-what-you-do God-love. *Agape* love is how God loves you and me in Jesus Christ. It's a perfect verb-love. It continues to love even when we fail to feel it. It remains solid even when our feelings shift, even when we are uncertain or unaware of it.

Are you and I capable of loving with *agape*? I'm not sure we can ever reach that high on the love scale. But that's the love Jesus calls us to strive to reach. *Agape* is the love that allows us to love those who hate us and those who hurt us. *Agape* is the love that keeps us showing love to the trusted friend who betrays us, to the unloving husband who abandons us, to the irresponsible mother who deserts us, to the disgraceful father who abuses us, to the wily church member who takes advantage of us, to the lust-filled employer who harasses us. Only *agape* can accomplish these feats, for it is supernatural love. *Agape* is God's love—

unconditional, persevering, purposeful, and perfect.

We can quote Paul's love poetry, found in 1 Corinthians 13, and not really understand its true meaning. Reread Paul's description of love, using *agape,* and see if it doesn't make the meaning clearer. I treasure the translation Eugene Petersen gives us in *The Message*. He paraphrases:

> If I speak with human eloquence and angelic ecstasy but don't have love, I'm nothing but the creaking of a rusty gate.
>
> If I speak God's Word with power, revealing all his mysteries and making everything plain as day, and if I have faith that says to a mountain, "Jump," and it jumps, but I don't love, I'm nothing.
>
> If I give everything I own to the poor and even go to the stake to be burned as a martyr, but I don't love, I've gotten nowhere. So, no matter what I say, what I believe, and what I do, I'm bankrupt without love.
>
> Love never gives up.
>
> Love cares more for others than for self.
>
> Love doesn't want what it doesn't have.
>
> Love doesn't strut,
>
> Doesn't have a swelled head,
>
> Doesn't force itself on others,
>
> Isn't always "me first,"
>
> Doesn't fly off the handle,
>
> Doesn't keep score of the sins of others,
>
> Doesn't revel when others grovel,
>
> Takes pleasure in the flowering of truth,
>
> Puts up with anything,
>
> Trusts God always,
>
> Always looks for the best,
>
> Never looks back,
>
> But keeps going to the end.

Impossible Love?

What is the opposite of *agape*? Selfishness. Francis Schaeffer described selfishness as "two impoverished values that grow out of . . . radical individualism." Society's "radical individualism" lusts after

1. personal peace, which means just to be let alone, not to be troubled by the troubles of other people . . . to live one's life with[out] being disturbed;
2. affluence, which means an ever-increasing prosperity, a life made up of things and more things; success is judged by an even higher level of material abundance.[1]

Jesus talked about *agape*:

> You have heard that it was said, "Love your neighbor and hate your enemy." But I tell you: *Love your enemies and pray for those who persecute you,* that you may be sons of your Father in heaven. . . . If you love those who love you, what reward will you get? Are not even the tax collectors doing that? And if you greet only your brothers, what are you doing more than others? Do not even pagans do that? Be perfect, therefore, as your heavenly Father is perfect. (Matthew 5:43–48, emphasis mine)

"Praying for his or her enemies distinguishes the Christian from everyone else," writes Don Aycock. "It is appropriate behavior for followers of Jesus. Praying for an enemy . . . gives something back for the coming generation because it helps break the cycle of hate and fear. It's *tough*! But it's necessary."[2]

We must somehow *pray* for our enemies and *love* our enemies—something almost humanly impossible to do. The kind of love Jesus describes here is "verb-love," love in action. My friend Gerald Austin, pastor of an inner-city church ministry, writes, "We must commit ourselves to loving our neighbors. The Lord wants us to see:

- "Love is not limited by its object." Verb-love can *love* actively and completely even when the object of that love is undeserving of that love.

- "Love is demonstrated by action." Verb-love has little to do with our personal feelings and everything to do with our personal actions—how we demonstrate and practice love toward other human beings.

- "Love must be intentional." Verb-loving someone is no accident. It takes effort, energy, time, and purpose. We must be intentional when we show verb-love to another in need.

- "Love will cost you something." Consider what verb-love cost Jesus—His life.

Consider what verb-love cost His mother, Mary—the embarrassment of her pregnancy as a single woman, and the death of her Son.

Consider what verb-love cost the Good Samaritan—his money, his wine, and his time (see Luke 10:25–37).

Verb-love is expensive love, love that we spend out of our own pain and pockets in order to reach out, love, and help our neighbor in need.[3]

Verb-love is selfless. It always puts others first. It reaches out and loves even the unlovely. According to Paul, verb-love "never gives up" but "keeps going to the end." According to Jesus, verb-love even "loves enemies" and "prays for those who persecute you." Verb-love loves the rebellious teenager who selfishly holds out his hand for more money and cares nothing for the future of his family. Oh, how richly Shakespeare captured this ungrateful prodigal: "Sharper than a serpent's tooth is the thankless child!" But the loving Father loves even the unlovely boy. He waits by the window and looks far into the distance watching for the familiar gait of his beloved son. When the loving Father sees the repentant son, He runs out to meet him—this boy who smells of sweat and swine. He welcomes him back into the family and throws a party to celebrate his return.

Jesus used this story to show the Father's unconditional verb-love. When the boy's money ran out, he ended up working in the pigpen—a lower than low place for a Jewish boy to work!

> [Keeping swine] was considered one of the most degrading employments, not only by the Jews, but by other nations. Among the Egyptians, for example, the swineherd was completely shut off from society. The Saviour makes use of this antipathy to illustrate the depth of misery to which the dissipation of the young prodigal had brought him.[4]

As I said before, love is not a feeling but an action. We can love our enemies because love is not something we *feel* but something we choose to *do*. Love is a kindness extended to someone who doesn't deserve that kindness. Genuine love—Christ's *agape*—can motivate us to do things for others that we would never consider doing otherwise!

This is love beyond human affection. When we love others, especially the "unlovely," we move beyond mere human love. We love them with God's love. God's love allows us to *see* the world with His eyes, to *love* humanity with His heart, and to *reach out* with His hands to those who hurt. That's *agape, divine gift-love.*

"Divine gift-love in the man enables him to love what is not naturally lovable; lepers, criminals, enemies, morons, the sulky, the superior and the sneering."[5]

Verb-love—the love that loves even those who hurt and persecute you—is the love that was shown by Heather Mercer and Dayna Curry when they volunteered their lives to serve God among the war-torn women and children in Afghanistan. As a college student at Baylor University in Waco, Texas, Heather prayed that God would send her to the "hardest place on earth." And He did.

Heather talks about verb-love when she writes, "I came to

realize that my love for God would be directly expressed through my service to the poor. Love had to be demonstrated—how could it be authentic otherwise?"[6]

Heather chose to demonstrate her love for God by going to Afghanistan. The Taliban arrested Heather and her fellow relief worker, Dayna Curry, for talking about Jesus to Afghanistan's Muslim people. They were placed in a mice-infested, filthy prison in Kabul, where the young women endured 105 days of harsh captivity. During this time, on September 11, 2001, Muslim terrorists, masterminded by Osama bin Laden, hijacked four U.S. planes and attacked both the World Trade Center towers in New York City and the Pentagon in Washington, D.C., killing thousands of people. Still imprisoned when President George W. Bush declared war on "terrorism," Heather and Dayna sang praises to God and prayed during America's bombing raid on Afghanistan. They slept under their cots at night as bombs exploded above their prison cell. In the evenings, before the bombing began, Dayna went outside in the prison courtyard to pray and worship God. Those quiet times of personal worship helped Dayna hold on to her verb-love for the Muslim people, the Taliban officials, and the prison guards: "These times of quiet in God's presence brought me the strength and peace I needed to endure the strain. As I reflected on my life, I was able to let God heal me of deep hurts and open my eyes to His goodness."[7]

Verb-love is such a deep, beautiful, unselfish love. I find it hard to understand and to comprehend. Yet verb-love is the kind of unconditional love God calls each believer to practice. Sometimes our verb-love can even mean the difference between life and death for us, or for those we love.

Verb-love is love in action, even when no one knows it. The greatest account of verb-love is John 3:16: "For God so loved the world that He gave His only begotten Son, that whoever believes in Him should not perish but have everlasting life." God had this kind of love for you and me when He willingly gave His only Son to die on the cross.

Oh, how He loved His only Son, arrested by soldiers, spit upon, and mocked. But there was only one thing to do. A world of people were speeding through time and space, passing through the centuries, and they had only Him to save them from eternal destruction.

As the cross was lifted and thrust into the ground, God heard the agonizing cries of His Son as Jesus hung by nailed hands and feet and died a slow, painful death. No one saw the tears on God's face. Few noticed or remembered the crushed, bruised body upon that wooden cross. And no one guessed the price just paid so that they might be saved.

Perfect Agape Verb-Love

What is verb-love? It's the kind of love that joins us to the loving Creator, that continues to call us back into His presence, back into the Quiet Place.

Verb-love is the Middle-Eastern father, forgetting his expected dignity, and running down the road to meet his son—the selfish boy who has drained the father's "IRA, savings account, and retirement fund." In ancient times, Middle-Eastern fathers did not run. We expect this father to punish his son, to make him a family slave, to make him sleep in the barn. But, you see, real love is a verb. It runs. It forgives. It welcomes the prodigal boy—still covered with pig dung—back into the family.

Verb-love is the Native-American grandfather ("Granpa") in the story of *The Education of Little Tree*. Little Tree is a poor young Cherokee boy who lives with his grandparents in the Tennessee mountains in the 1930s. One day, as he stretches out on the creek bank, hand-fishing in a mountain stream, the small boy hears a "dry rustle that started slow and got faster until it made a whirring noise."

"I turned my head toward the sound," remembers Little Tree.

"It was a rattlesnake. He was coiled to strike, his head in the air, and looking down on me, not six inches from my face."

Little Tree "froze still and couldn't move."

"He was bigger around than my leg and I could see ripples moving under his dry skin," he recalls. "He was mad. Me and the snake stared at each other. He was flicking out his tongue—nearly in my face—and his eyes was slitted—red and mean."

While the snake decides which part of Little Tree's face to strike, a shadow falls gently over them. It was Granpa.

"Don't turn yer head. Don't move, Little Tree," he says. "Don't even blink yer eyes."

As the snake raises his head and prepares to attack Little Tree, Granpa's big hand slips between the boy's face and the snake's fangs.

"The hand stayed steady as a rock . . . the rattler struck, fast and hard. He hit Granpa's hand like a bullet. . . . I saw the needle fangs bury up in the meat as the rattler's jaws took up half his hand."

A loving grandfather takes a snake's stinging bite—a bite meant for his grandson. Then, "Granpa . . . grabbed the rattler behind the head, and he squeezed. . . . Granpa . . . choked that snake to death with one hand, until I heard the crack of back-bone. Then he throwed him on the ground."

Granpa almost died from that snakebite. He took that snake's bite to save Little Tree from a painful death. That's verb-love.[8]

Verb-love is the old black deckhand, Timothy, in *The Cay*. Timothy saves the life of the arrogant white boy, Phillip, after their ship, *The Hato*, is torpedoed and sunk in Caribbean waters in April 1942. Timothy quietly takes the rich boy's kidding and disdain when both are washed up onto a deserted island. There is nothing to love about this spoiled, selfish boy who grumbles and complains and orders the black man to serve him. Yet Timothy teaches Phillip to sharpen a stick and to catch fish. He holds Phillip and comforts him when the boy is frightened. He shows the boy how to build a hut and a rain catchment. And then one day a deadly hurricane threatens to tear across the island, and Timothy unselfishly saves the boy from death.

Timothy sees the hurricane coming.

"Dis be a western starm, I b'guessin'," he says. "Dey outrageous strong when dey come."

When the storm hit, "there was a splintering sound, and Timothy dropped down beside me, covering my body with his," remembers Phillip. "Our hut had blown away. He shouted, 'Phill—eep, put your 'ead downg.' I rolled over on my stomach, my cheek against the wet sand."

As Timothy wraps his own big body around the boy, the rain "was hitting my back like thousands of hard berries blown from air guns," writes Phillip. "We stayed flat on the ground for almost two hours, taking the storm's punishment, barely able to breathe in the driving rain."

When the storm became violent, Timothy found a palm tree high on the island's hilltop.

"Standing with his back to the storm," Phillip remembers, "Timothy put my arms through the loops of rope, and then roped himself, behind me, to the tree."

For the endurance of the hurricane, Timothy takes the full blows of the storm, sheltering the terrified boy with his body.

"I could feel the steel in his arms as the water tried to suck us away," recalls Phillip.[9]

After the storm passes, Phillip unties the ropes and discovers that Timothy has been cut to ribbons by the wind. It has flayed the old man's back and legs. Timothy is dead. An old man's verb-love has saved the life of a spoiled boy.

"I buried Timothy," writes Phillip, "placing stones at the head of the grave to mark it. I didn't know what to say over the grave. I said, 'Thank you, Timothy,' and then turned my face to the sky. I said, 'Take care of him, God, he was good to me.' "[10]

Only Christ's verb-love allows us to reach out to unlovely

and unappreciative people. Only Christ's verb-love compels us to pray for those people who persecute us. Verb-love can only deepen within our own hearts when, through faithful prayer, we come to the Quiet, and move closer to the Giver of Love—God himself.

But verb-love is such a risk. Can anything hurt our heart and despair our soul more deeply than the betrayal of a friend, or the unfaithfulness of a spouse, or the deceit of a child? We open our hearts and souls to the possibility of pain beyond endurance when we love with God's love.

C. S. Lewis wrote,

> To love at all is to be vulnerable. Love anything, and your heart will certainly be wrung and possibly be broken. If you want to make sure of keeping it intact, you must give your heart to no one, not even to an animal. Wrap it carefully round with hobbies and little luxuries; avoid all entanglements; lock it up safe in the casket or coffin of your selfishness. But in that casket—safe, dark, motionless, airless—it will change. It will not be broken; it will become unbreakable, impenetrable, irredeemable. . . . The only place outside Heaven where you can be perfectly safe from all the dangers and perturbations of love is Hell.[11]

Selfless Divine-Gift Love

Let me share with you two stories of *divine-gift love* that will warm your heart. The first is about Rogelio and Yolanda Garcia and their son, Rogelio, Jr. Two decades ago, the Garcias left their small town in Mexico and moved to Los Angeles. One of three children, Rogelio, Jr., graduated from high school with all A's. He was a hard-working, smart student. He yearned to become an engineer. He dreamed of going to the Massachusetts Institute of Technology (MIT) in Cambridge, Massachusetts.

But the Garcias were poor. They had no money. They owned few possessions. No one in the entire Garcia family had ever been to college. So Rogelio and Yolanda planned a way to send their boy to MIT.

Late at night, after working a full day at their jobs, these loving parents piled into their old white truck and went to work collecting thrown-away tin cans in the back alleys of Los Angeles. They worked every night for years, collecting hundreds of thousands of cans to pay for their children's educations. On June 6, 2002, Rogelio and Yolanda watched their son, Rogelio, Jr., graduate with honors from MIT. That special graduation day was the first time since 1985 that Rogelio and Yolanda took a day off from searching for cans in dumpsters.

The Garcias left Cambridge a day ahead of schedule, for they have two more children, Angel, fifteen, and Adriana, twenty, to educate. Why did they leave early? Because "Saturday is our best [can-collecting] day," said Yolanda, "a tiny fifty-two-year-old whose smile glows brightly against dark cheeks tanned from so many years toiling under the California sun."[12]

Silas Purnell is another beautiful example of divine-gift love. Living in public housing on Chicago's South Side, Purnell, a black man, has helped thousands of inner-city kids, mostly disadvantaged blacks, through college. A seventy-eight-year-old energetic man, Purnell "would do almost anything to help them get an advanced education—pick up the phone and cajole a college administrator into accepting a bright but untested teen and wheedle some scholarship money out of them too; dig into his own wallet to help pay for books, bus fare to school or a pair of glasses; load up his station wagon with teens whose world view didn't extend beyond their gritty Chicago neighborhoods and drive them to distant campuses."

A former marketing manager for Coca-Cola, Purnell quit his job in the mid–1960s, cleaned out his basement to set up an office, and began helping kids who wanted to go to college. He worked seven days a week and has taken only two vacations in more than three decades. "Where others saw hopeless cases—teenagers held back by racism, poverty and history who 'didn't have the slightest idea' how to get into college—[Purnell] saw untapped potential."

"These kids, nobody placed any value on them. It was understood they'd grow up and be nothing," Purnell said. "I knew it didn't have to be that way."

One of the students, Quincy Moore, now forty-nine, earned a Ph.D. in counseling education, thanks to the generosity of Purnell. Moore is currently the dean of undergraduate studies at Westchester University outside Philadelphia.

"I owe a debt that I could never repay," Moore says.[13]

No doubt Moore expresses the deep appreciation felt by many more of Purnell's students!

WATCH OUT FOR PREJUDICE

Another form of hate that robs our soul of its God-given rest is racial prejudice. A universal problem, we see the devastating results of prejudice around the world.

After September 11 and the terrorist attacks, an ugly cloud of prejudice rose over the United States. Fear causes prejudice, and Americans feared another attack by Muslim terrorists led by Osama bin Laden. Anyone with Middle-Eastern physical features became suspect. For a while fear and prejudice ran rampant throughout the streets of America. One Saturday, shortly after the terrorist attacks, Balbir Singh Sodhi, forty-nine, from Punjab, India, was landscaping the grounds around his Mesa, Arizona, gas station. A member of the Indian Sikh community, with his traditional long beard and turban, Sodhi somewhat resembled the men of Afghanistan. In what was later called "a crime of hate and revenge," Francisco Roque, forty-two, shot Sodhi, the father of three children, to death. Many Sikhs believed Sodhi was the first to be killed in retaliation for the World Trade Center and

Pentagon attacks. Police arrested Roque and held him on a $1-million bond.

Sodhi was not the only victim of hate crimes in the United States during the week after the attacks. The Council on American-Islamic Relations received more than three hundred reports of harassment and abuse.

A man in Queens, New York, was shot in the forehead by a BB gun as he left a temple. He had gone there to pray for the World Trade Center victims. Another man, in Fairfax, Virginia, was nearly driven off the road by two vans. He was on his way to donate blood for injured victims. A Hindu temple was fire-bombed in New Jersey. Sikh Dharma's official Web site reported 133 incidents of hate crimes in the few days after September 11.

Attacks on Muslim-Americans were also reported. Mosques in Irving and Denton, Texas, were attacked. In Cleveland, Ohio, a man rammed his car into a mosque, causing some $100,000 in damage. Some Muslims in Washington State were afraid to go to their mosques.

Racial hate has no place. We must not vent our anger on innocent Americans just because they might physically resemble Osama bin Laden or the people of Afghanistan. "Muslim-Americans need to be treated with respect," stated President Bush after he learned of these acts of prejudice.

We can combat prejudice and hate with love and generosity. During the days after the attacks, Christians took unequalled opportunity to show Christ's love in action. We witnessed repeated acts of love in those post–9/11 days. We saw groups of Americans gather to pray. People formed long lines to donate blood. New York City was overwhelmed with donations of food and clothes and cash. Caring people from around the nation volunteered their time to help others at the "Ground Zero" disaster site. In spite of the incidences of racial prejudice, the huge outpouring of love by compassionate people was constant throughout this tragedy.[14]

Jesus saw much hate in His day too. Perhaps that is why He spoke a great deal about love. As far as hate crimes go, not much has changed in two thousand years. Jesus told His disciples, "A new command I give you: Love one another. As I have loved you, so you must love one another. By this all men will know that you are my disciples, if you love one another" (John 13:34–35).

Gandhi—A Hero in Prejudiced Times

One man who fought racial prejudice was Mahatma Gandhi. I have long admired the life and work of this man, the "Father of the Nation" of India. Born in 1869, he was a "man of iron will" and "moral sensibility" who embarked upon a "relentless search for truth." Gandhi was a Hindu, not a Christian, and that is unfortunate. Had Gandhi become a Christian, he might have won the entire country of India to Christ.

Once in England, during his school years, Gandhi met a Christian friend in a vegetarian boarding house. This new friend introduced the young Gandhi to the Bible. Gandhi struggled through the Old Testament, but he "fell in love with the New Testament, especially Jesus' Sermon on the Mount."

Gandhi's seeking heart was moved by this message. Why didn't he make a commitment to Christ and become a Christian? Largely because of racial prejudice.

As a young man in South Africa, Gandhi tried to enter a church building to hear the missionary C. F. Andrews speak about Christ. He had heard much about Andrews, and he wanted to meet and talk with him. But because of his brown face, Gandhi was not allowed in the building. Would Gandhi have accepted Christ had the church allowed him to enter its doors and hear the missionary? We will never know. Soon after that experience, Gandhi "rejected Christianity and went on to lead 400,000,000 people as a Hindu." E. Stanley Jones, commenting on Gandhi's experience with prejudice, wrote,

"Racialism has many sins to bear, but perhaps its worst sin was the obscuring of Christ in an hour when one of the greatest souls born of a woman [Gandhi] was making his decision."[15]

Gandhi later admitted that he was tempted to become a Christian, and he might have become a Christian, had it not been for Christians![16]

Segregation

I now live in Birmingham, Alabama, where so much civil unrest took place for many years. I have placed my hands on the very bars that imprisoned Martin Luther King, Jr., when he wrote his infamous "Letter From a Birmingham Jail." Oh, the pain this city once produced and experienced because of powerful, ugly prejudice! I see such an effort now among Christian leaders and church members here to right the past wrongs of racial hatred and prejudice. It now seems impossible that our society could be so divided because of skin color.

I grew up in Atlanta, Georgia, during the days that Martin Luther King, Jr., marched for peace and renounced bigotry and hatred. I remember the public water fountains and the rest rooms that were marked "for coloreds" and "for whites only." I watched the evening news, and I saw the fire hoses and clubs and police dogs attack people because of the color of their skin. I went to church, and I never saw an African-American in the pews; nor in my public schools; nor in my neighborhood.

I spent a good portion of my childhood and youth in a state of confusion. My parents weren't particularly prejudiced; it was just that society on the whole was filled with racial hatred. During church on Sunday mornings, we learned to "love our neighbor." But after the worship service, my family, as well as many other church families, often ate at Lester Maddox's famous Atlanta restaurant, "The Pickrick." No person of color was allowed to eat there. I remember the prejudiced jokes and hateful laughter that blended with the fried chicken and peach cobbler as we waited in the long cafeteria line for our food. I also remember how Maddox advertised and sold his "souvenir ax handles" in the front of the restaurant. They came in different sizes—in order to "beat" black people of different ages—from kids to adults. I also remember the frightening KKK marches—the mobs of that invisible cowardly army of hate in the white robes and pointed hoods with slits cut out for eyes.

In those days, Montgomery, Alabama, was the center of racial prejudice and injustice in the United States. When Rosa Parks made her courageous decision not to move to the back of the bus, a young minister, Martin Luther King, Jr., only twenty-six years old, was thrust into the Civil Rights Movement. That's when the threats from the Klan began. They threatened to shoot King, to firebomb his house. King was arrested and thrown into jail. A bomb exploded on his front porch and filled his home with smoke and broken glass.

How easy it would have been for him to quit the fight. He could have stepped out of the ring and allowed hatred and racial prejudice to continue to thrive. But King had had a taste of God's love from God himself. King became an example of *agape* as he sought to "love his enemies" and "to pray for those who persecuted" him and others.

Verb-love cost King his life. More than three decades ago, on April 4, 1968, one day after my seventeenth birthday, a white man shot and killed Martin Luther King, Jr. Verb-love cost Coretta Scott King her husband, and her children their father. But verb-love is expensive love—it costs us something. Sometimes it costs us our very lives.

On the day King was killed, Dolphus Weary, a black student who attended Los Angeles Baptist College, wrote, "I remember running to my room, flipping on the radio, and listening to the news report. A rifle bullet had ripped into King's neck as he stood on a motel balcony in Memphis, Tennessee. . . . I was devastated. As I sat on my bed holding back the tears, I heard voices down the hall: white students talking about King's shooting." But Weary quickly realized that they weren't just talking—they were laughing.

"I couldn't understand what I was hearing," Weary says. "These Christian kids were glad that Dr. King—my hero—had been shot." So confused, Weary admits, "I had to ask God how to respond."

Deep inside, Weary wanted to hate white people. "But then I remembered," he said, "the heart of Dr. King—responding to hate with love." Instead of hating, Weary rechanneled his anger into working hard to build genuine relationships with his white peers, in order to "take every opportunity on that campus to help those young minds think differently." Weary responded with love—Christ's love—verb-love.

"I think that is the way Dr. King would have approached it," he says. "King's heart was to look at the broader picture. The small picture is to be angry. The broader picture is to devote yourself to changing the system and changing minds. That was King's great work. . . . He came along and told us that we're all created in God's image, and that we ought to start looking at each other as brothers and sisters, especially those of us in the Christian church."

"We must keep God in the forefront," King said. "Let us be Christian in all our actions. . . . Love is one of the pinnacle parts of the Christian faith. There is another side called justice, and justice is really love in calculation."[17]

A contemporary of mine, author Philip Yancey, also grew up in Atlanta in the midst of racial disharmony and civil rights marches led by Dr. King. Although I've never met Philip Yancey, I have read all of his books, and I can identify with many of his early memories about Southern racism. He writes about some of his personal experiences in the article "Confessions of a Racist," first published in *Christianity Today* on January 15, 1990:

Today I feel shame, remorse, and also repentance. . . .
It took years for God to break the stranglehold of blatant
racism in me—I wonder if any of us gets free of its more
subtle forms—and I now see this sin as one of the most
poisonous, with perhaps the greatest societal effects.

The real goal, King used to say, was not to *defeat* the
white man, but "to awaken a sense of shame within the
oppressor and challenge his false sense of superiority." . . .
The end is reconciliation; the end is redemption; the end
is the creation of the beloved community. And that is
what Martin Luther King, Jr., finally set into motion, even
in diehard racists like me.

Only *agape* can overcome racial prejudice. It is God's love that
"never gives up," but "keeps going to the end." God's love is the
proud Middle-Eastern father's blistered feet and forgotten dignity.
It is the Native-American grandfather's snake-bitten, poisoned
hand.

It is the old black man's life-saving, bleeding back.

It is the twenty-six-year-old pastor's fight for freedom that
cost him his life.

What is verb-love? It is the *agape* of God that reaches down
to us through Jesus Christ, comforts our hearts, and gives rest to
our souls.

Chapter Fourteen

RESTING OUR SPIRIT

Hate and prejudice—these are two sin-separators that take root in our heart and soul and lead us far away from the rest of the Quiet Place. These destructive weeds strangle our intimacy with God and with each other. But love—God's *agape*, His verb-love—conquers both hate and prejudice, enriching our lives and the lives of many others, bursting into beautiful blooms that lead to peace.

Bitterness and selfishness also starve and stunt our spiritual growth. They bring unrest to those around us—in our family, in our community, and in our church. God's family has no room for bitterness, which is based on unforgiveness. It also has no room for selfishness, which comes from a lack of compassion for others.

BITTERNESS

When Mary's husband of twenty years left her for another woman, abandoning both her and their two children, she grew bitter. She hated him. She hated his new wife and her children. For two years Mary allowed bitterness to fester within her heart and soul. She agonized over the divorce, his betrayal, and his indifference to her and the children. As a Christian, Mary knew she couldn't harbor bitterness in her heart. She knew that her bitterness damaged her intimacy with God. She knew she had to forgive her husband for his betrayal.

"I looked in the mirror one day, two years after the divorce, and I said, 'Mary, you are a bitter *young* woman.' I could see lines of hatred and bitterness already creasing my face. Then I decided right there to forgive my husband and his new wife. I didn't want to look into that same mirror years from now and see a bitter *old* woman!"

Mary chose to forgive. She depended on God to help her when she felt the reoccurring taste of bitterness revisit her heart. And God did indeed help Mary. Several years later Mary knew she had truly forgiven her ex-husband and his new wife. She became deeply at peace and depended more than ever on God's love to fill her soul and keep her from future bitterness.

Forgiveness will possibly be the hardest thing you and I will ever have to do! But it is something we *must* do if we are to protect our heart and soul from bitterness. I have learned that forgiveness is not a natural human response. When we've been wounded, we naturally want to take revenge on the person who hurt us. In ancient days, Moses' law addressed those people who were wounded by another person. The "eye for an eye and a tooth for a tooth" law might sound cruel, but Moses gave this law to protect the offender from possible murder. The offender might lose an eye, but the law would save his life (see Exodus 21:24; Leviticus 24:20; Deuteronomy 19:21).

Unforgiven

One of the saddest stories I've ever read happened in Poland in 1944. Simon Wiesenthal, who was previously a Jewish inmate in a Polish concentration camp, is sent on cleanup duty to a makeshift hospital for German soldiers. When Wiesenthal arrives, a nun takes him to the room of a dying twenty-one-year-old Nazi named Karl. Karl, one of Hitler's SS men, asks Wiesenthal to hear his confession. Karl yearns to seek the forgiveness of a Jew for his part in the Nazi war crimes against the Jewish people.

While Wiesenthal listens, Karl confesses to setting fire to a building and burning alive hundreds of Jewish men, women, and children crammed inside. He recalls one particular family who died that day. Their soot-smeared faces have haunted Karl since the murders.

Wiesenthal hears Karl's story. He is drawn to the authenticity of Karl's confession, but he is also repelled by the horrifying tale. Karl "indicates that he wants to die in peace, and that he has longed to talk about [his crime] to a Jew and beg forgiveness from him."

Wiesenthal's heart is moved by this miserable dying man. But he is unable to forgive Karl.

"At last," Wiesenthal writes, "I made up my mind and without a word I left the room."

Wiesenthal later agonized about his decision and wondered: "Ought I to have forgiven him?" The question of forgiveness haunted Wiesenthal for the rest of his life.[1]

How can a Jewish man forgive a German soldier who helped Hitler exterminate millions of Jewish people? We see the effects of hatred and prejudice around the world today. How can we possibly forgive those people who murder, rape, rob, and ruin others? Does God really intend for us to forgive those militants who hijacked our jets and crashed them into our skyscrapers, killing thousands of people?

"In *Shoah*, Claude Lanzmanns' documentary on the Holocaust, a leader of the Warsaw ghetto uprising talked about the bitterness that remains in his soul over how he and his neighbors were treated by the Nazis. He writes, 'If you could lick my heart, it would poison you.' "[2]

Unforgiveness, and the bitterness that results, will poison you and me—heart, mind, and soul. Researchers are discovering that unforgiveness is bad for our physical, mental, and emotional health. Forgiveness, on the other hand, actually fosters our good health.

"While the Biblical practice of forgiveness is usually preached as a Christian obligation," writes Gary Thomas, "social scientists are discovering that forgiveness may help lead to victims' emotional and even physical healing and wholeness."[3]

When We Choose to Forgive

When we choose to forgive the one who has hurt us, our forgiveness can bring an eternal result. Kari Schneider admits the bitterness in her heart when her Christian husband of nine years, Larry, told her he no longer loved her. Only hours after his bombshell statement, Kari went into labor and delivered her second daughter. When Kari and her newborn arrived home, her husband packed his suitcases and left. Kari discovered later that Larry was having a sexual affair with his secretary. Larry hired a lawyer and finalized the divorce.

Larry started dating another woman, Lisa, a verbally abusive mother of a preschooler. Kari found herself hating both Larry and Lisa.

"My hatred toward them both was venomous," she said.

Kari's life went downhill. She, too, turned away from God, and had an affair as well as a bout with alcohol. After a long hate-filled struggle that left her guilt-ridden and ashamed, Kari came back to her faith in God.

"God revealed the answer," she said. "I had too much unforgiveness in my heart. I knew [God] wanted me to forgive the entire cast of characters in my nightmare. . . . While it was difficult, I managed to forgive them."

Kari struggled with forgiveness: "It was the hardest thing I'd ever tried to do," she admits. After Kari forgave them, she asked

God to help her "love" them, especially Lisa. She started spending time with Lisa and ministering to her when she had surgery. Through Kari's love and prayers, Lisa came to the Lord, gave Him her life, and prayed for her own personal forgiveness. Kari had the opportunity not only to witness to Lisa, but to disciple Lisa in Bible study for one year.

Later in her life, God led Kari to reach out to other people consumed with bitterness from divorce. She started a divorce care group at her church. Kari's many acts of forgiveness changed her life, Lisa's life, and the lives of many others consumed with bitterness.[4]

When we refuse to forgive another person, our spiritual lives become rest-less. A wide gap forms between us and God. Bitterness separates you and me from the very One who forgives us, His erring children.

"When there is a gap between me and Christ," wrote Mother Teresa, "when my love is divided, anything can come to fill the gap. Confession is a place where I allow Jesus to take away from me everything that divides, that destroys."[5]

George Herbert writes, "He that cannot forgive others breaks the bridge over which he himself must pass if he would ever reach heaven; for every one has need to be forgiven."[6]

A Time to Mend

The writer of Ecclesiastes tells us, "There is a time for everything, and a season for every activity under heaven. . . . A time to *tear* and a time to *mend*" (see Ecclesiastes 3). The ordinary living of everyday life can *tear* apart relationships, friendships, and marriages. Perhaps you are dealing with a torn relationship. Maybe someone has deeply hurt you. If so, come to the Quiet Place, and let God teach you how to *mend* a torn relationship. Allow God to help you forgive the person who has injured you, so that nothing will stand in the way of your own personal prayers and loving friendship with God. Forgiveness takes place in our hearts, in our souls, and in our lives. And forgiveness starts in the Quiet Place.

What does forgiveness mean? The word *forgive* means "to pardon." For illustration's sake, take a piece of chalk and scribble on a clean blackboard. Think of your messy scribbling as a friend or spouse's hurtful actions toward you, ugly offenses you didn't deserve. Now take an eraser and completely erase all the scribbles from the blackboard. You have just erased those offenses. You have "forgiven" your friend or spouse for his or her hurtful actions toward you. Whether they deserve your forgiveness or not, you have pardoned them. Whether they asked for your forgiveness or showed remorse for their actions, you have still forgiven them. You no longer hold the resentment or bitterness against them. You have chosen to release them from their debt of sin. That's complete forgiveness. That's complete pardon.

Gustavo Gutierrez writes,

> Pardon is an inherent characteristic of the Christian community. To pardon means not to fixate [on] the past but to create possibilities for persons to change and to re-align the course of their lives. . . . Pardon forges Christian community.[7]

As Roman soldiers crucify Jesus, He prays, "Father, forgive them, for they do not know what they are doing" (Luke 23:34). Jesus forgives those men who nail his hands to the beams, who thrust a spear in His side, and who laugh and mock Him at His feet.

Jesus insists that we follow His example, that we also forgive others. He says,

> Forgive us our debts, as we also have forgiven our debtors. . . . For if you forgive men when they sin against you, your heavenly Father will also forgive you. But if you do not forgive men their sins, your Father will not forgive your sins. (Matthew 6:12, 14)

All of us who struggle, or have struggled, with forgiveness know that forgiveness usually takes much prayer and much time. "God can forgive in a single breath," writes C. S. Lewis. "But we need time." Before he died, Lewis wrote, "I think I have at last forgiven the cruel schoolmaster who so darkened my youth. I had done it many times before, but this time I think I have really done it."[8]

When forgiveness takes place, the person doing the forgiving discovers a newfound peace. Love begins to penetrate the bitter human heart. Our burden becomes light; our yoke becomes easy. Peace and joy are the results of a forgiving heart. I, as a Christian woman, must learn to forgive as I have been forgiven.

The apostle Paul writes, "Bear with each other and forgive *whatever grievances* you may have against one another. Forgive as the Lord forgave you" (Colossians 3:13, emphasis mine). What does "whatever grievances" include? Every sin committed against you, including a deceitful husband or an ungrateful child or a cruel schoolmaster.

John also reminds us that God has forgiven all our sins when he says, "If we confess our sins, He is faithful and just and will forgive us our sins and purify us from all unrighteousness" (1 John 1:9). God forgives us our sins in an ongoing process. It is in the Quiet Place that we ask God's forgiveness for our own wrongdoings. And it is in the Quiet Place that we learn the beauty of forgiving others.

Selfishness

Another sin-separator that damages our relationship with the Lord is selfishness. What is the solution to selfishness? Compassion—sincere compassion that reaches out in Christ's love to others.

Paul encourages us to "clothe [ourselves] with compassion, kindness, humility, gentleness and patience" (Colossians 3:12). I believe that *compassion*, like forgiveness, is not a normal, natural, or instinctive human emotion. It is a God-gift to His children, to those who dearly love Him. God shows His compassion through us when we are willing and eager to put an end to our selfishness, to love and reach out to help others. Jesus showed the ultimate compassion for you and me. So intense a compassion, so intense a love, it led Him to the Cross.

Jesus knew compassion.

> To learn how God views suffering on this planet, we need only look at the face of Jesus as he moves among paralytics, widows, and those with leprosy. In contrast to others in his day, Jesus showed an unusual tenderness toward those with a history of sexual sins—witness his approach to the Samaritan woman at the well, the woman of ill repute who washed his feet with her hair, the woman caught in the act of adultery. In Jesus, said [John] Donne, we have a Great Physician "who knows our natural infirmities, for he had them, and knows the weight of our sins, for he paid a dear price for them."[9]

Compassion means "to suffer with" or "to suffer alongside of." When we offer compassion to a friend, we offer our heart to her. When she is troubled, our own heart is troubled. When she cries out in pain, we too cry out in pain. Compassion embraces our friend and tells her she is not alone in the dark valley. She has two "friends" with her—you, and her eternal Friend, Jesus.

"Compassion is born when we discover in the center of our own existence not only that God is God and man is man, but also that our neighbor is really our fellow man."[10]

I love to see genuine loving compassion between people. The selfless compassion and generous love shown by the American people after the 9/11 terrorist tragedy overwhelmed the rest of the world. How refreshing to see this outpouring of love from a secular society that has so long known narcissism, not niceness;

chaos, not kindness; crime, not community; meanness, not meekness; hate, not hospitality; slavery, not sympathy; selfishness, not sharing; greed, not gentleness; harshness, not helpfulness; lust, not love; confusion, not compassion! When we show compassion to another, we show compassion to Jesus himself.

Mother Teresa said that "when she looks into the face of a dying beggar in Calcutta, she prays to see the face of Jesus so that she might serve the beggar as she would serve Christ."[11]

Believers have long known how God feels about compassion. "The Lord is compassionate and gracious, slow to anger, abounding in love," writes the psalmist.

"Because of the Lord's great love we are not consumed, for His compassions never fail, they are new every morning," writes the author of Lamentations.

Throughout the Gospels, we see the loving compassion of Jesus. Matthew writes that Jesus went through all the towns and villages, teaching and preaching and healing disease and sickness. When Jesus saw the crowds of hurting people, He had compassion on them, "because they were harassed and helpless, like sheep without a shepherd."

"The Lord is full of compassion and mercy," writes James.

And who can ever forget the compassionate, loving Jesus as He overlooks the city of Jerusalem in Matthew 23: "O Jerusalem, Jerusalem, you who kill the prophets and stone those sent to you, how often I have longed to gather your children together, as a hen gathers her chicks under her wings, but you were not willing."

Throughout Jesus' ministry, He constantly reached out to hurting people with heartfelt compassion.

He showed compassion to the sick throughout Galilee, healing all who were ill with various diseases, those suffering severe pain, the demon-possessed, those having seizures, and the paralyzed (Matthew 4:23–25).

He touched and cured a man with leprosy—the incurable

"AIDS" of the ancient world (Matthew 8:1–4).

He healed the servant of a Roman centurion in Capernaum (Matthew 8:5–13).

He cooled a fever from the brow of Peter's mother-in-law (Matthew 8:14–15).

Jesus was constantly reaching out with health and life and tender compassion to those who hurt—a paralytic (Matthew 9:1–8); a bleeding woman (Matthew 9:20–22); a dead girl (Matthew 9:23–26); the blind and the mute (Matt. 9:27–33); the hungry crowds (Matthew 15:32–38); to a demonized boy (Matthew 17:14–18); an earless servant of the high priest (Matthew 26:50–54); blind Bartimaeus (Mark 10:46–52); dead Lazarus (John 11:1–44); Nicodemus (John 3:1–21); and Zacchaeus (Luke 19:1–10).

By His gracious example, Jesus shows you and me how to reach out to hurting people with His loving compassion.

Women today are hurting. I meet them everywhere I go. I see the pain in their faces. I hear the hurt in their voices. You and I must reach out, tell them how to find the Quiet Place, so that they too can discover God's rest and healing for their souls.

I sat down one day during my prayer time and thought deeply about women and the difficulties they suffer. I made a list that grew and grew until I ran out of room to write. Consider some of the many problems that women in today's society face: abortion guilt, spousal abuse, unresolved anger, caretaking of others, childbirth, child-rearing, parenting, depression, divorce and separation, abandonment, aging and loss of youth, beauty and energy, exhaustion, unrealistic expectations from others, financial worries, credit debt, sexual abuse in childhood years, grief, handicaps, health problems, health insurance, isolation, loneliness, legal problems, loss of loved ones, marriage problems, in-law conflicts, blended marriage challenges, physical-emotional-spiritual pain, onset of menopause, miscarriage, personality disorders, rejection, low self-esteem, sexual problems, shyness, stress,

substance abuse, concerns over retirement, time management difficulties, obesity, eating disorders, lack of work skills, lack of education. . . .

No doubt you can think of many more that I've failed to list.
Women today need the love and compassion of those who spend
time in the Quiet Place. Those who have felt the touch of God's
own compassion are the ones equipped to reach out with His
compassion to others who are hurting. Surely genuine compassion is learned firsthand in the silence and solitude of the Quiet
Place.

I believe the four major sin-separators that hinder our prayer
relationship with God are hate, prejudice, bitterness, and selfishness. It is in the Quiet Place that you and I learn the solutions
that restore rest to the soul and prayer to the heart. Love relieves
hate and prejudice. Forgiveness melts bitterness. Compassion
overcomes selfishness.

Many other things can interfere and strangle our relationship
with God. If we fail to guard our hearts, they can also cause us
great unrest and keep us far away from the Quiet Place. We, as
Christian women and wives and mothers, must constantly be
aware of our natural tendencies toward pride, selfish ambition,
worry, disobedience, love of money and/or possessions, deceit,
dishonesty, and other sin-separators. Think about the damage we
do to ourselves spiritually when we allow sin-separators to live
uninterrupted in our hearts and souls. They rob us of Christ's joy
and rest in our lives, and they kill our intimacy with God.

Chapter Fifteen

FINDING NURTURE AND NOURISHMENT

One of my spiritual mentors is Brother Lawrence, a monk born in 1611, who spent his life working in the monastery's kitchen in Paris. In the midst of steaming pots, noisy pans, and clanging dishes, Brother Lawrence practiced the presence of God. No matter how noisy the kitchen became or how many monks passed through and interrupted his private worship, Brother Lawrence communed without ceasing with the Lord he so loved. Somehow Brother Lawrence

> learned to cultivate the deep presence of God so thoroughly in his own heart that he was able to joyfully exclaim, "I am doing now what I will do for all eternity. I am blessing God, praising Him, adoring Him, and loving Him with all my heart." . . . It is God who paints Himself in the depths of our soul. We must merely open our hearts to receive Him and His loving presence.[1]

This monk loved peace and quiet and solitude, yet for some reason God placed him in the busy and noisy and chaotic monastery kitchen! What did he do? He found the Quiet Place within his own heart and soul, and there he continually communed with God. His heart became his chapel, and he lived there deep within the Quiet.

Perhaps you, like me, long for silence and solitude, yet find yourself surrounded by interruptions, requests, emergencies, and general restless noise. How many times I have longed to return to Kappal, the quiet monastery high upon the Swiss mountaintop. But again, most of us don't live in twelfth-century monasteries where we can lose ourselves in the sacred silence of the Quiet Place. We are involved from head to toe in the busyness of life in today's harried society. How can you and I, in the clang and clamor of an ordinary day, guard our heart and allow God to nurture our soul? Here are some suggestions.

Make Your Heart a Chapel

We don't have to be sitting or kneeling in church in order to pray. God lives only a whisper away. We can come to His Quiet Place within our own hearts and commune with Him there. Brother Lawrence reminds us, "It isn't necessary that we stay in church in order to remain in God's presence. We can make our heart a chapel where we can go anytime to talk to God privately."[2]

And there, in your private chapel, get to know God. Brother Lawrence said,

> We have to know someone before we can truly love them. In order to know God, we must think about Him often. And once we get to know Him, we will think about Him even more often, because where our treasure is, there also is our heart.[3]

Meditate on God's Word

We can find the answers to our faith-questions within the pages of Scripture. Allow God's Word to be your guidebook for life, for it is a miracle book, inspired by God himself.

Imagine the divine dynamics God designed to give us His Word between the covers of one book! The word *Bible* means "books" or "scrolls."

How should we approach the Bible?

- As the inspired Word of God (2 Timothy 3:16; Hebrews 1:1);
- As the inspired Word of the Holy Spirit (2 Peter 1:21; Acts 1:16);
- As the sacred book that presents Christ.

How do we find understanding as to the meaning of Scripture?

- Through the work of the Holy Spirit (1 Corinthians 2:14–15; Psalm 119:18).

Why should we trust Scripture?

- Because it is a gift from God to us;
- Jesus trusted the Scriptures as God's authoritative Word (Matthew 19:4; 22:29);
- Paul and the apostles believed the scrolls to be the "very words of God" (Romans 3:2).

How have believers considered God's Word in the past?

- As the "Word of Christ";
- As the "Word of Life";
- As the "Word of Truth";
- As a two-edged sword that is not to be added to or taken from;
- Not to be handled deceitfully;
- To be searched and studied and taught;
- To be read publicly.

The *Westminster Confession* of 1646 says:

> The authority of the Holy Scripture, for which it ought to be believed and obeyed, depends not upon the

testimony of any man or church, but wholly upon God (who is truth), the Author thereof; and therefore it is to be received, because it is the Word of God.

What does Scripture tell us about itself?

- "All Scripture is God-breathed and is useful for teaching, rebuking, correcting and training in righteousness, so that the man of God may be thoroughly equipped for every good work" (2 Timothy 3:16–17);
- "The unfolding of your words gives light; it gives understanding to the simple" (Psalm 119:130);
- "Heaven and earth will pass away, but my words will never pass away" (Matthew 24:35);
- "Your Word is a lamp to my feet and a light for my path" (Psalm 119:105);
- "The Word became flesh and made his dwelling among us. We have seen his glory, the glory of the One and Only, who came from the Father, full of grace and truth" (John 1:14).

What are we supposed to do with God's Word?

- "Do your best to present yourself to God as one approved, a workman who does not need to be ashamed and who correctly handles the word of truth" (2 Timothy 2:15);
- "Let the word of Christ dwell in you richly as you teach and admonish one another with all wisdom" (Colossians 3:16);
- "If you remain in me and my words remain in you, ask whatever you wish, and it will be given you. This is to my Father's glory, that you bear much fruit, showing yourselves to be my disciples" (John 15:7–8);
- "I have hidden your Word in my heart that I might not sin against you" (Psalm 119:11).

Dr. W. A. Criswell, in his book *Why I Preach That the Bible Is Literally True*, writes that the Bible is the literal, inspired, God-breathed truth of heaven, the book that reveals to us truth that is able to bring us into living union with God. Jesus read and quoted the Bible as verbally inspired.

Imagine how the Bible came into being! The Bible contains sixty-six books written by forty different men. It was written on two continents, in countries hundreds of miles apart. The Bible was written in deserts, wildernesses, caves, tents, prisons, and palaces. It was written in three different languages (Hebrew, Aramaic, and Greek). The first part of the Bible was written 1,500 years before the last part was written. It took sixteen centuries to write the Bible!

It was written by people of every level of political and social life—from a king on his throne to a shepherd in his field to a fisherman on the sea. It was written both by educated princes and poets and philosophers and physicians to fishermen and tax collectors. Yet Criswell acknowledges the Bible is one complete organic unity and whole. Every part of the Bible fits every other part. There is one ever-increasing, ever-growing, ever-developing plan pervading the whole. It contains one system of doctrine, one system of ethics, one plan of salvation, and one rule of faith. There is a perfect harmony throughout the Scriptures from the first verse in Genesis to the last verse in Revelation. It is a masterminded book! A living book! It has challenged people for thousands of years—even though entire civilizations and governments have tried to destroy it. It is still the number-one bestseller![4]

I greatly miss W. A. Criswell since his recent death. I've enjoyed many wonderful conversations with this great preacher over the years. When we spoke, he called me "daughter." I liked that. His genuine love for God's Word proved contagious.

God's Word, the Bible, is a *living book*—a personal, intimate letter from God to you and me (Hebrews 4:12). Let us make a place and a time each day to read, study, and reflect upon God's Word.

Seek Silent Places

I often seek out quiet places where I can meditate and pray without interruption or schedule. I find that silence nurtures my soul. I come back to my busy world refreshed after I sip Jesus' living water. The quiet has a calming effect on my soul.

Jesus sought silence. He was in the silence of the wilderness for forty days and forty nights, thinking, praying, and communing on a deeper level with His Father. The Middle-Eastern wilderness is deadly and desolate, home to poisonous snakes and scorpions. The ancients believed demons lived among the jagged, barren hills. It's a scary place. But Jesus needed the stillness and isolation of the wilderness. He wanted to pray and to seek God's guidance.

Jesus often trekked to the mountains to find a quiet place. Sometimes He climbed into a little boat and pushed himself away from the crowded shores and onto the beautiful Sea of Galilee. He wanted to embrace the silence and the solitude so that He could pray, seek the will of His Father, and have His tired soul refreshed.

Jesus often spent whole nights alone in the Quiet and in prayer. He rose often before daybreak to speak with God in the silence and solitude of the early morning while the world around Him slept (see Mark 1:35). If Jesus so needed the stillness of silence and solitude, how much more do you and I need the Quiet Place! Never feel guilty because your heart yearns to leave home and hearth to seek Jesus. Never pass up the opportunity to commune with Christ at the deeper level that silence and solitude provide.

Mother Teresa was right when she said, "We cannot put ourselves directly in the presence of God if we do not practice internal and external silence. . . . Silence gives us a new outlook on everything. . . ." The compassionate nun suggested that we "listen in silence because if your heart is full of other things you cannot hear the voice of God."[5]

As we have seen, silence in our society is hard to find.

> In reality, silence is almost nonexistent. If we stop speaking and turn off our telephones and televisions and radios and computers, there is always some sound of technology at work, nearby or far off. A refrigerator humming. An airplane droning overhead. A truck straining up a hill.[6]

Even though you must sometimes search for silence, diligently seek it with all your heart.

Allow God's Natural Beauty to Soothe Your Soul

Some of my most memorable personal worship times happen when I am surrounded by nature's beauty. Jesus often meditated in green gardens (see Mark 14:35, where He prayed in the Garden of Gethsemane). He withdrew to the beauty of the mountains (see Matthew 17, where He was transfigured before Peter, James, and John, and Mark 3:13–19 when, on the mountainside, Jesus chose His disciples). He sought the loveliness of the lake (see Mark 3:7). When the world around Him became too chaotic, Jesus left the scene, found a quiet spot in nature, and allowed God to replenish His soul.

Not long ago, after a hot, tiring day of visiting various Middle-Eastern religious sites, I, too, found a pocket of nature that nourished my soul. Sitting on the grass, in the same area where Jesus preached the Sermon on the Mount, I felt the wind off the Sea of Galilee blow through my hair. I feasted my eyes on the deep-blue lake waters. I drank in the lush green trees and grass and wildflowers that grew around me on that beautiful hillside. I listened to the silence. And I thought how this same hillside and lake and gentle breeze and these trees, grass, and wild flowers must have refreshed Jesus' own tired soul. The lush, green hills around the Sea of Galilee proved a wonderful place to rest—both for me and for Jesus.

What great beauty God has given us. I once tried to explain the gorgeous colors of nature to my dear friend Helen Parker. Born blind, Helen couldn't conceive of color. I described God's paintbrush strokes of greens and blues and pinks, how the white stars twinkled against the canvas of the black night sky, how each morning's sunrise turned the palate of the heavens to peaches and cream. I longed for Helen to "see" my verbal rainbow, the arch set high in the afternoon sky, the soft hues each distinctive in color yet blending so beautifully together. I tried to help Helen understand the beauty of tiny yellow buttercups dotted across a lawn of green. The indescribable effort made me stop and ask myself, *Why did God give us the beauty of nature and color?* and *When the nonbeliever basks in nature's beauty, to whom does she say thank you?*

Sister in Christ, spend time in God's natural world. Learn to fish, hike, swim. Take long walks. Buy some in-line skates. Ride a bike. Seek out woods and lakes and mountainsides. The beauty will refresh your soul. And there in the midst of the growing colors, step into the Quiet Place and rest.

Seek Your Sacred Place of Stillness and Solitude

"Solitude seeks to silence a noisy world. But it is also a tool to quiet our souls, which are often wracked by their own inner turmoil, tensions, and troubles."[7]

Visit your place of sacred solitude often, for it is "a place where your mind can be idle, and forget its concerns, descend into silence, and worship the Father in secret. There can be no contemplation where there is no secret."[8]

How God yearns for us to slow down, to "Be still, and know that [He is] God" (Psalm 46:10).

Rest

Jesus tells us, "Come unto Me, and I will give you rest." Oswald Chambers wrote,

> It is after we have begun to experience what salvation means that we surrender our wills to Jesus for rest. Whatever is perplexing heart or mind is a call to the will— "come unto Me." It is a voluntary coming. . . . The whole of the life after surrender is an aspiration for unbroken communion with God.[9]

God's very presence promises rest. The writer of Exodus recorded (in 33:14): "My Presence will go with you, and I will give you rest."

Create of Serenity a "Quiet Knowing"

"A quiet knowing is . . . a sense of serenity," write Gigi Graham Tchividjian and Ruth Bell Graham.

> Most people I know are desperately searching for a sense of serenity. Serenity is that inner peace that comes with the certainties of knowing in whom you believe, what you believe, who you are, and where you're going. . . . "A quiet knowing" comes through a personal relationship and deep intimacy with God through Jesus Christ. . . . It is being always and forever conscious of His encircling presence.[10]

Serenity also comes from knowing what we can control and what we must give up to God and allow Him alone to control. In 1934 Reinhold Niebuhr prayed a special prayer in a worship service at a small church in Heath, Massachusetts. After the service, Harold Chandler Robbins, a summer neighbor, asked Niebuhr for a copy of the beautiful prayer. Today we know the prayer as the "Serenity Prayer":

God, grant me the serenity
To accept the things I cannot change,
Courage to change the things I can,
And wisdom to know the difference. Amen.

These twenty-five simple words, prayed from the heart and practiced by the soul, can change a life.[11]

Step Into the Moment and Enjoy It Fully

I often hear myself saying the happiness-strangling phrase "One of these days, I will. . . ." Instead of enjoying the moment in which I presently live, I am dreaming deeply about some vague future moment. My friend Paula looked me directly in the eye one day and said, "Hey, Denise, *this is the future!*" She was right.

Have you ever found yourself living in a "future" that doesn't exist and may never happen? I have:

"I'll take that trip when my baby gets out of diapers."

"I'll lie down and rest when I have more time."

"As soon as I finish spring-cleaning this house, I'll have some fun."

"Next summer I'll invite my friends to lunch."

"After I retire from my job, I'll write a book."

"One of these days I'm going to start enjoying life."

Friend, let me tell you something that both you and I already know. We are not guaranteed the future. We might not even live through the night. I don't mean to sound morbid, but it is a fact. The future is now. This present moment. Live it or relinquish it. You won't get a second chance to relive this moment. Some of the real tragedies of the World Trade Center attack were the missed kisses good-bye, the I-love-you's not said, the final hugs not given. Be aware of life and love. Live life today, in this very moment.

Lose yourself and your sense of time. Notice what is happening around you, and drink in the beauty of the present moment.

One day your son's tiny baby feet will be wearing size-ten shoes. Your friend will move to another state. You will be reading your late husband's will. You will be cleaning out your parents' home. Take a mental snapshot while you bask in those special life moments. And reflect on them often.

> Get a life in which you notice the smell of salt water pushing itself on a breeze over the dunes, a life in which you stop and watch how a red-tailed hawk circles over a pond and a stand of pines. Get a life in which you pay attention to the baby as she scowls with concentration when she tries to pick up a Cheerio with her thumb and first finger. Turn off your cell phone. Turn off your regular phone, for that matter. Keep still. Be present.[12]

Pray Without Ceasing

Seek to learn how to practice the presence of God in your everyday life. How do we practice the presence of God?

> By remembering Him, praising Him, asking for His grace, offering Him your troubles, or thanking Him for what He has given you will console you all the time. During your meals or during any daily duty, lift your heart up to Him, because even the least little remembrance will please Him. You don't have to pray out loud; He's nearer than you can imagine.[13]

Pray without ceasing, as the apostle Paul urges us to do in 1 Thessalonians 5:17.

Pray in Secret

While Jesus prayed publicly on occasion, He most often prayed in private. Catherine Marshall wrote,

> How Jesus loved to pray in secret Himself! He had a habit of "rising up a great while before day" and going

outdoors—to a mountainside or some other deserted place—to pray. Perhaps because of the small, crowded Palestinian houses, that was the only way He could find privacy and solitude.[14]

The times Jesus chose to pray publicly, He prayed aloud for the benefit of His listeners. He prayed out loud before He took five loaves and two fish and fed five thousand: "Taking the five loaves and the two fish and looking up to heaven, *He gave thanks* and broke the loaves" (Mark 6:41, emphasis mine). Jesus wanted the people to glorify God for providing their lunch.

Jesus prayed publicly when He raised Lazarus back to life. Here again, He allowed those around Him to hear His loud prayer so that they would credit the Father with the miracle of new life. Listen: "Father," Jesus said in a loud voice, "I thank you that you have heard me. I knew that you always hear me, but I said this for the benefit of the people standing here, that they may believe that you sent me" (John 11:41–42).

Another time Jesus prayed out loud served to benefit His disciples. How fortunate we are today to have recorded for us Jesus' beautiful prayer found in John 17. He prays this prayer specifically for the ears of His disciples and for our ears today.

Mostly, however, Jesus prayed in secret places, in silence and solitude, away from the maddening crowds.

"The key to communication with God is secret prayer. If you spend time in the secret place, you will exude peace in the midst of life's storms."[15]

Jesus recommends that we pray in secret. In His day, the religious leaders [Jesus called them "hypocrites"] prayed out in the open where people could see and hear them. They stepped up on their public stages and performed their prayers. When the Pharisees prayed, it was show time!

In reaction to these performances, Jesus told His followers to hide themselves in closets, to pray without an audience, to forego the public's praise and applause, and to pray in secret (Matthew 6:5–6). He also told believers to give to the needy in secret (Matthew 6:1–4) and to fast in secret (Matthew 6:16–18). When we pray, give, and fast in secret, our Father in heaven will reward us.

When we pray from the secret places of our heart, we need not use words.

"While we have a tendency to view prayer as speaking to God, insights often come in quietness. Just waiting, being silent, is often the most effective way of praying."[16]

Martin Luther agreed with the method of wordless prayers. "The fewer words, the better prayer," he said.

Chapter Sixteen

THE TRANSFORMATION OF OUR SOUL

Our Savior, our Lord, our Jesus calls to you and to me. Listen. Do you hear Him? "Come to Me, all you who labor and are heavy laden, and I will give you rest" (Matthew 11:28 NKJV). "Take my yoke upon you and learn from me, for I am gentle and humble in heart, and you will find rest for your souls. For my yoke is easy and my burden is light" (Matthew 11:29–30).

Jesus waits by our side, ever-present to transform our mind, our body, our heart, and our soul with His divine gift of rest.

Come to Him in solitude. Solitude means "being out of human contact, being alone, and being so for lengthy periods of time."[1]

Come to Him in silence. "Silence means to escape from sounds, noises, other than the gentle ones of nature."[2]

Come to Him in quiet prayer. "In the silence of the heart God speaks. If you face God in prayer and silence, God will speak to you. . . . Souls of prayer are souls of great silence."[3]

Come to Him in repentance.

As we gradually gain more insight into ourselves, we

are able, with God's grace, to find ways to resist habitual sin and grow in self-control. We gain strength bit by bit, like an athlete striving for the prize. Gradually we reclaim more and more of ourselves and offer it to God's trans-forming light. Thus the Holy Spirit works within us, sanctifying us from the inside out.[4]

Come to Him with mind, body, and spirit.

We are not only mind (thought and emotions) and body, but we are also spirit. Our spirit is the part of our being that resonates with beauty, shows compassion to the wounded, lambastes evil, and reaches upward for a rela-tionship with the Creator. Through our personal spirit God the Father teaches us, communicates with us. . . . When our personal spirit is nurtured through communion with God, worship, and exposure to beauty our whole being flourishes.[5]

Come to Him in honesty.

Human withdrawal is a very painful and lonely pro-cess, because it forces us to face directly our own condi-tion in all its beauty as well as misery. When we are not afraid to enter into our own center and to concentrate on the stirrings of our own soul, we come to know that being alive means being loved.[6]

Come to Him in humility.

Humility is not the same as resisting the urge to show off (which is modesty) or denying that you have gifts and talents (which is lying). Humility is remembering that you have a beam in your eye. In every situation remember what God knows about you, and how much you have been forgiven. . . . Account yourself the "chief of sinners" and be gracious toward the failings of others.[7]

Come to Him believing.

For feelings come and feelings go,
now feelings are deceiving.
My warrant is the word of God,
not else is worth believing.
Though all my heart should feel condemned
for want of some sweet token,
there is One greater than my heart
whose Word cannot be broken.[8]

Come to Him and seek His face.

Do you have a place of shelter where you seek only His face? Do you spend time in that secret place? Have you given prayer the priority it deserves? When you pray, remember it is the Lord's face you seek.[9]

Come to Him for peace.

God offers us divine peace. Divine peace is a deep inner confidence in God. In fact, it is possible to have the peace of God even in the midst of war. Divine peace is not dependent on outside circumstances. It can flourish even when external circumstances are absolutely the worst they can be.[10]

Come to Him for transformation. "If we mature spiritually, we also will be increasingly transformed into Christ's image" (Romans 8:29).[11]

Come to Him for rest. " 'Hesychia' is the Greek word for rest . . . this perfect rest of body and soul."[12] "Rest. Rest. Rest in God's love. The only work you are required now to do is to give your most intense attention to His still, small voice within."[13]

Dear sister in Christ, come to the Quiet, for it is there that Jesus waits for you and offers you His deep communion. Come to the Quiet, for it is there that Jesus teaches you the secrets of solitude and rest.

I treasure this time I've spent with you. Thank you for journeying with me throughout the pages of this book. I hope God's Word, written within these chapters, has blessed you and encouraged you. Life is not easy. But Jesus shares your yoke.

As I write these final words, my prayer for you is this:

The Lord bless you and keep you;
The Lord make his face shine upon you
And be gracious to you.
The Lord turn his face toward you
And give you peace.
(Numbers 6:24–26)

Study Guide

For Personal and/or Group Use

The following study guide can be used for your personal enrichment or used with a group for discussion. Perhaps you and a friend, spouse, prayer partner, or child can work on these questions together. Answer only the ones you feel comfortable answering. May this simple study guide enrich your personal and/or shared study of God's Word.

Some Questions to Ponder and Answer:

Introduction: Exhaustion and the Twenty-First-Century Woman

1. "Exhaustion has become the new look of the twenty-first-century woman." Do you believe this? Why or why not?
2. What is your definition of "rest"?
3. In your opinion, why would a Christian woman "feel guilty" about taking time to rest?
4. Do you consider rest a luxury or a necessity? Why?
5. Describe the Proverbs 31 woman in terms of work and wisdom.
6. Why must we, as women, learn the importance of "divinely appointed rest"?
7. Consider the following question: Why do we live such an "ironic existence, complaining about how tired and overwhelmed we feel, but refusing to accept the gift of rest God offers?"

Chapter 1: Mama's Shoulder

1. Describe a time in your life when you felt truly rested. Where were you? Describe the depth of your rest. What do you remember about that time?

2. Ponder the following statement: "The person who wants to arrive at interiority and spirituality has to leave the crowd behind and spend some time with Jesus."

3. What does Jesus mean by His statement "I am the way and the truth and the life. No one comes to the Father except through me" (John 14:6)?

4. What is "soul-rest" as defined in this chapter?

5. Scott Savage writes, "We come into this world created in God's image, but we also share in the consequences of humanity's fall from grace in our natural propensity to sin." Do you believe this statement? Why or why not?

6. What did Eugene O'Neill mean when he said, "The grace of God is glue"?

7. In Philip Yancey's *What's So Amazing About Grace*, how does he describe "grace"?

Chapter 2: Our Minds—Created for the Quiet

1. Describe a time when you took a retreat to a quiet, lonely place. Where did you go? What effect did the rest have on your mind?

2. What happens to you mentally when you seek the Quiet Place?

3. Have you been able to share a "moment of Quiet" with someone who needed it? Describe the experience.

4. Read Matthew 11:28 in several different translations and ponder it.

Chapter 3: Mind Attack!

1. What is the "noise level" of your home life?

2. Describe the "invasion" the English villagers of 1898 endured in H. G. Well's *The War of the Worlds*.

3. Contemplate this statement: "The truth is that the dangers to which we are most vulnerable are generally not the sudden, dramatic, obvious ones. They are the ones that creep up on us, that are so much a part of our environment that we don't even notice them." Do you agree or disagree?

4. Explain what happened to Scott and Mary Ann when they gave up their complicated lives and moved into a quiet Quaker community in Barnesville, Ohio. Have you ever wanted to leave the "world" behind and find a quieter place to live? Tell about it.

5. What kinds of things did Scott notice when he gave up his car and started to walk?

6. Describe your most worshipful worship experience. What made it so special?

Chapter 4: Resting Our Mind in Christ

1. What does it mean to "rest your mind in Christ"?

2. Ponder this statement by Charles Swindoll: "It doesn't require a Ph.D. from Princeton to assess that we are busy, busy, busy. Forever on the move, doing things, eating stuff, working. . . ." Do these words describe your life?

3. In what ways could you change your life in order to spend more time with Christ in the Quiet? Are you willing to make these changes?

4. What does John Updike mean when he says, "Our brains are no longer conditioned for reverence and awe"?

5. What is the effect of television on your home life? Your family life?

6. What are some of your own personal suggestions for making your home and office a quieter, more restful place?

7. What does the apostle Paul mean (in Philippians 4:7) when he writes, "The peace of God, which transcends all understanding, will guard your hearts and your minds in Christ Jesus"?

8. What advice does Paul give us in Philippians 4:8? Why is this advice important?

Chapter 5: Letting Christ Transform Our Mind

1. What does it mean to "develop an attentiveness to God's voice in us"?

2. How can we learn to "live in awareness of God's existence"?

3. In what ways will Christ transform our minds if we ask Him to?

4. What does Henri Nouwen mean when he writes, "We do not take the spiritual life seriously if we do not set aside some time to be with God and listen to Him"? Do you agree or disagree?

5. Ponder this statement: "Without solitude it is virtually impossible to live a spiritual life. Solitude begins with a time and place for God, and Him alone."

6. Paul writes, "Let this mind be in you, which was also in Christ Jesus." What does he mean by this statement?

Chapter 6: Today's Woman—Overworked!

1. Can you personally relate to the issues surrounding women and work? What is your own work situation?
2. Do you try to live under the unrealistic American "have it all, do it all" expectations for women today?
3. Do you sometimes feel overwhelmed with your current workload?
4. How often do you stop and think through your work priorities? What have you discovered?
5. Do you agree with Dr. James Dobson when he writes, "Families are in worse shape now [than in previous years]. . . . And [they are] steadily deteriorating"? Why or why not?
6. Have you ever suffered from "vacation starvation"? Describe the situation.
7. Henri Nouwen writes, "Our lives often seem like overpacked suitcases bursting at the seams. In fact, we are almost always aware of being behind schedule." Do you ever feel like this? Describe.
8. Do you agree that "busyness has become a sign of importance"? Why or why not?
9. From what source do you personally derive your sense of self-worth?
10. Why are so many women today leaving the workplace?

Chapter 7: Stress Attack!

1. What is stress?
2. What is the difference between "crisis stress" and "everyday stress"?
3. What happens to your body when you feel stressed?
4. Susan Zarrow writes, "You can expect to become just as ill with these repeated, daily aggravations [everyday stress] as you would from major, life-changing traumas [crisis stress]." Do you agree? Why or why not?
5. What are the pressures in your life that send you into feelings of "dis-stress"?

6. What changes can you make in your life to help keep stress under control?

Chapter 8: *Job Stress*

1. What is "job stress," and how does it personally affect you?
2. Why are working women today so susceptible to "job stress"?
3. Do you agree with Charles Swindoll when he says that "work is fast becoming the American Christian's major source of identity"? Why or why not?
4. Have you seen in yourself, or others, evidence of overwork, fatigue, overexpectations from others, and feelings of inadequacy? In what ways can these everyday stresses make a woman sick?
5. Do you work at a stressful job? Describe your work situation.
6. Describe what is meant by "commute cancer." Are you a victim of this?
7. What is meant by the term "work daze"?
8. Ponder this statement by Arthur Gish and discuss or consider: "It . . . seems as if our society were designed to break the human spirit. Rather than a style of life, it might be called a style of death."

Chapter 9: *Majoring in the Minors*

1. What does it mean to "major in the minors"?
2. Stop and ask yourself, "What is the meaning of this short life?" Write down your answer.
3. Describe Jesus' work habits. Did He leave a credible work example for us to follow today?
4. What is the difference between "earth's treasures" and "heaven's treasures"?
5. Joseph Girzone writes, "Not that [Jesus] was condemning the possession of things, but the distraction and the craving for them which simulates the worship and attention we should reserve only for God." Do you agree with this statement? Why or why not?
6. What lessons can we learn from Guy de Maupassant's story *The Necklace*?
7. Do you agree or disagree that "style is a major ingredient of the emptiness in modern culture"?

8. Read John 17:4 and apply Jesus' words to your own life and work philosophy.

Chapter 10: De-Stressing and Resting Our Body

1. What suggestions would you give the Christian woman who works outside her home and stays exhausted from her work?
2. Why should we, as Christian women, think through our priorities?
3. Do you strive to create regular times and spaces to meet with God?
4. Do you, like many other women, have difficulty in saying no when someone asks you for help?
5. Are you trying to "live in the present moment" and "live one day at a time"?
6. What does it mean to "simplify and de-clutter your life"? In what specific ways have you done this?
7. Why is money considered "one of the most unsatisfying of possessions"?
8. Why is it important to take care of your physical body? How do you do this? What advice would you give to other women?
9. Why is it important that women not smoke?
10. In what ways do you deal with "dis-stress" in your life?
11. In what ways do you "calm the 'hurry' rhythm" of your body?
12. Do you suffer from the "habit of hurry"? How does it affect your personal life and your family's life?
13. Do you have a support group of trusted friends? Why is this so important?
14. Look at the Holmes/Masuda "Social Readjustment Rating Scale." Honestly assess your life. Add up your points. Are you above or below the level of "dis-stress"?

Chapter 11: Transforming Our Body

1. Why is solitude so vital to our physical health?
2. What is the value of physical rest?
3. Describe how God rested on the seventh day of Creation.
4. What does Jesus tell us and show us about resting our bodies?
5. What does *sabbatismos* mean? What does *anapausis* mean?
6. Why is "rest and solitude" needed in the "cycle of life for women

as they seek to revive their physical energies"? What opportunities does rest afford us?

7. Read 1 Kings 19, the story of Elijah. How did food, water, and rest revive him to continue God's work?

Chapter 12: Yoked With Heavy Burdens

1. Describe what Scripture means by the words *heavy laden* and *burdened*.

2. What is a yoke? How does it work?

3. Ponder the following biblical stories. Compare the problems of the first-century woman with the problems of the twenty-first-century woman. Are they similar? If so, in what ways?

- The Samaritan woman Jesus encounters at Jacob's well (John 4:1–42).
- The woman caught in adultery (John 8:1–11).
- The bleeding woman (Mark 5:25–34).
- The crippled woman (Luke 13:10–17).
- The financially burdened widow whose only son died (Luke 7:11–17).

4. Describe Jesus' dying words to John concerning His mother (John 19:26–27).

Chapter 13: Guarding Our Heart

1. What are the "sin-separators" you are dealing with today?

2. How can we combat hate in our lives?

3. What is Hollywood's definition of "love"?

4. What is God's definition of "love"?

5. How are the two definitions of "love" different from each other?

6. Define "verb-love."

7. C. S. Lewis wrote, "Divine gift-love in the man enables him to love what is not naturally lovable; lepers, criminals, enemies, morons, the sulky, the superior and the sneering." Do you agree with him? Why or why not?

8. Name some examples about selfless acts of love and compassion that you have witnessed or heard.

9. Did you find a common element in each of the stories of love and compassion that were presented in this chapter?

Chapter 14: Resting Our Spirit

1. What "sin-separators" are exposed in this chapter, and how can they "take root in our heart and soul, and lead us far away from the rest of the Quiet Place"?

2. How can bitterness and selfishness starve and stunt our spiritual growth?

3. What is the cure for bitterness?

4. What is the cure for selfishness?

5. What decision about forgiveness would you have made if Karl had asked you, instead of Wiesenthal, for forgiveness? Do you think Wiesenthal made the right decision? Why or why not?

6. What did George Herbert mean by the following statement: "He that cannot forgive others breaks the bridge over which he himself must pass if he would ever reach heaven; for every one has need to be forgiven"?

7. Scripture tells us that Jesus was constantly reaching out with tender compassion to those who hurt. Look up in God's Word and read aloud the following examples: a paralytic (Matthew 9:1–8); a bleeding woman (Matthew 9:20–22); a dead girl (Matthew 9:23–26); the blind and the mute (Matthew 9:27–33); the hungry crowds (Matthew 15:32–38); a demonized boy (Matthew 17:14–18); an earless servant of the high priest (Matthew 26:50–54); blind Bartimaeus (Mark 10:46–52); dead Lazarus (John 11:1–44); Nicodemus (John 3:1–21); and Zacchaeus (Luke 19:1–10).

8. What are some of the problems that today's women face? How can we, as Christian women, reach out and help others who are hurting?

Chapter 15: Finding Nurture and Nourishment

1. Who was Brother Lawrence? How did he "practice the presence of God"?

2. Brother Lawrence reminds us that "it isn't necessary that we stay in church in order to remain in God's presence. We can make our heart a chapel where we can go anytime to talk to God privately." How can we "make our heart a chapel"?

3. Why is the Bible called a "miracle book"? Why should you and I trust God's Word?

4. Why is internal and external silence so important to the nurture and nourishment of our spirit?

5. How can God's natural beauty around us soothe our souls? How did Jesus respond to nature?

6. What do Tchividjian and Graham mean by "a quiet knowing"?

7. How can Christian women learn to "live in the present moment"? Why must we learn this art?

8. Is it possible, in your opinion, to "pray without ceasing"? Why or why not?

9. Reread the following Scriptures: Matthew 6:5–6; Matthew 6:1–4; and Matthew 6:16–18. What does Jesus tell us about the importance of the "secret place" when we commune with and serve God?

10. Do you have a Quiet Place where you can meet God in secret?

Chapter 16: The Transformation of Our Soul

1. Ponder Jesus' words in Matthew 11:28–30. What do they mean to you personally?

2. How should we come to Jesus? What is meant by the following advice?

- Come to Him in solitude.
- Come to Him in silence.
- Come to Him in quiet prayer.
- Come to Him in repentance.
- Come to Him with mind, body, and spirit.
- Come to Him in honesty.
- Come to Him in humility.
- Come to Him believing.
- Come to Him and seek His face.
- Come to Him for peace.
- Come to Him for transformation.
- Come to Him for rest.

ENDNOTES

Introduction

1. I am using *spirit* as a synonym for *soul*. The two terms are interchangeable in the context of this book.
2. Diane Passno, *Feminism: Mystique or Mistake?* (Wheaton, Ill: Tyndale, 2000), 113.
3. Dorothy Kelley Patterson, *BeAttitudes for Women* (Nashville: Broadman & Holman, 2000), 203.
4. John Anthony Page, "The Gift of Sabbath," *Discipleship Journal*, Issue 127, Jan./Feb. 2002, 34.

Chapter 1

1. Quoted in Richard J. Foster and Emilie Griffin, *Spiritual Classics* (San Francisco: HarperSanFrancisco, 2000), 149.
2. Ibid., 150.
3. Ibid., 151.
4. Scott Savage, *A Plain Life* (New York: Ballantine Books, 2000), 51.
5. Quoted in Philip Yancey, *What's So Amazing About Grace?* (Grand Rapids, Mich.: Zondervan, 1997), 270.
6. Scott Savage, *A Plain Life,* 51.
7. Philip Yancey, *What's So Amazing About Grace,* 71.
8. Brennan Manning, *Ruthless Trust* (San Francisco: HarperSanFrancisco, 2000), 26.
9. From "Frankenstein: Penetrating the Secrets of Nature," National Library of Medicine, online, n.d.
10. Mary Shelley, *Frankenstein,* first published in 1818, new edition published in 1992 by Penguin Books, London, 95–96.
11. Ibid., 97, 213.
12. Walter A. Elwell, ed., *Evangelical Dictionary of Theology* (Grand

Rapids, Mich.: Baker, 1984), 100.
13. John Donne.
14. C. S. Lewis, *The Four Loves* (New York: Phoenix Press, 1960), 188.
15. From *Holman Concise Bible Dictionary* (Nashville: Broadman & Holman, 1997), 558.
16. T. W. Hunt and Melana Hunt Monroe, *From Heaven's View* (Nashville: Broadman & Holman, 2002), 26.

Chapter 2

1. Quoted in Charles Swindoll, *Simple Faith* (Dallas: Word Publishing, 1991), 163, emphasis mine.

Chapter 3

1. "Cruel and Unusual Punishment," editorial, *Cincinnati Post,* 8 March 2002. Quoted from Chuck Colson's *BreakPoint,* Commentary #020419 (19 April 2002), "Cruel and Unusual?" *Turn-Off-TV-Week.*
2. H. G. Wells, *The War of the Worlds* (Harmondsworth, Middlesex, England: Penguin Books Ltd., 1986; first printing 1898), 85.
3. Ibid., 3.
4. Ibid., 72.
5. Ibid., 102.
6. Ibid., 59.
7. Ibid., 110.
8. Ibid., 55.
9. John Ortberg, *The Life You've Always Wanted* (Grand Rapids, Mich.: Zondervan, 1997), 90.
10. Scott Savage, *A Plain Life* (New York: Ballantine Books, 2000), 95.
11. Ibid., 150.
12. Ibid., 126.
13. Ibid., 120.
14. Ibid.

Chapter 4

1. Charles Swindoll, *Simple Faith* (Dallas: Word Publishing, 1991), 222.

2. John Updike, quoted in Philip Yancey, *The Bible Jesus Read* (Grand Rapids, Mich.: Zondervan, 1999), 27.

3. Allen Bloom, *The Closing of the American Mind,* quoted in Larry Burkett, *Women Leaving the Workplace* (Chicago, Ill.: Moody Press, 1995), 169.

4. Ibid., 168. "Adverse Health Effects of Noise," information from: *www.who.int/environmentalinformation/Noise/Comnoise–3.pdf www.macalester.edu/psych/whathap/UBNRP/Audition/site/noiseeffects.html*; *www.city.toronto.on.ca/health/hphe/pdf/noiserptattachmentmarch23.pdf*

5. Catherine Marshall, *Adventures in Prayer* (Grand Rapids, Mich.: Baker/Chosen Books, 1975), 65.

6. Joseph Cardinal Bernardin, *The Journey to Peace* (New York: Doubleday, 2001), 33.

7. Quoted in John O'Neil, "Performance: A Quick Power Nap's Benefits," *New York Times* online (28 May 2002).

Chapter 5

1. T. W. Hunt and Melana Hunt Monroe, *From Heaven's View* (Nashville: Broadman & Holman, 2002), 28.

2. Paul Brand and Philip Yancey, *In His Image* (Grand Rapids, Mich.: Zondervan, 1984), 129.

3. Roger Sperry, quoted in ibid., 128–29.

4. Leonard Sweet, *The Jesus Prescription for a Healthy Life* (Nashville: Abington Press, 1996), 88.

5. Eric Chaisson, *The Life Era* (New York: W. W. Norton, 1989), 253–54, quoted in William V. Pietsch, *The Serenity Prayer Book* (San Francisco: HarperSanFrancisco, 1990), 99–100.

6. "Teaching a Machine to Think," *Technology & Science* online, 2002, Associated Press.

7. Brand and Yancey, *In His Image,* 127.

8. Ibid., 132–33.

9. Henri J. M. Nouwen, *Making All Things New* (New York: Phoenix Press, Walker and Company, 1981), 72.

10. Ibid., 71.

11. Ibid., 69.

Chapter 6

1. Karl Rahner, quoted in Richard J. Foster and Emilie Griffin, *Spiritual Classics* (San Francisco: HarperSanFrancisco, 2000), 219.

2. Henri J. M. Nouwen, *Can You Drink the Cup?* (South Bend, Ind: Ave Maria Press, 1996), 100.

3. From *www.cnn.com*, *Larry King Live* interview with Dr. James Dobson of Focus On the Family (6 June 2002).

4. Faith Popcorn, *Dictionary of the Future* (New York: Hyperion, 2001), 365–66.

5. Chuck Colson's *Breakpoint*, "The Divorce Disaster," Nov. 2000, 19.

6. From cnn.com, *Larry King Live* interview (6 June 2002).

7. Colson's *Breakpoint*, "The Divorce Disaster," 19.

8. Maggie Gallagher, *The Abolition of Marriage*, quoted in Chuck Colson, *Answers to Your Kids' Questions* (Wheaton, Ill.: Tyndale House, 2000), 135.

9. Ibid., 136.

10. Genaro C. Armas, "Census: Unmarried Couples Increase," Associated Press, May 15, 2001.

11. Eric Schmitt, "Nuclear Families Drop Below 25 Percent of Households for First Time," *New York Times* online (15 May 2001).

12. Louis Uchitelle, "Women Forced to Delay Retirement," *New York Times* online (26 June 2001).

13. Ibid.

14. Ibid.

15. Nouwen, *Making All Things New*, 23.

16. Nouwen, *Can You Drink the Cup*, 99.

17. Diane Passno, *Feminism: Mystique or Mistake?* (Wheaton, Ill.: Tyndale House, 2000), 170.

18. Nouwen, *Making All Things New*, 25.

19. Hunt and Hunt Monroe, *From Heaven's View*, 23.

20. *Fortune* (27 June 1994), quoted from Larry Burkett, *Women Leaving the Workplace* (Chicago: Moody Press, 1995), 22.

21. Burkett, *Women Leaving the Workplace*, 33.

22. Ibid., 14.

23. Ibid., 51.
24. Ibid., introduction.

Chapter 7

1. Quoted by Richard J. Foster and Emilie Griffin, *Spiritual Classics* (San Francisco: HarperSanFrancisco, 2000), 160.
2. Wayne E. Oates, *Managing Your Stress* (Indianapolis: Bierce Associates, Inc., 1983), 3.
3. Anne Morrow Lindbergh, *The Gift From the Sea* (New York: Vintage Books, 1965), 96.
4. Patricia Van Tighem, *The Bear's Embrace* (New York: Pantheon Books, 2001), 16–18.
5. Ibid., 18.
6. Susan Zarrow, "Stress: The Facts," *Prevention* magazine, 39:9, Sept. 1987, 86.
7. From *www.stress.org/problem.htm*, "America's #1 Health Problem," from the American Institute of Stress, 124 Park Avenue, Yonkers, NY 10703.
8. Ibid.
9. Paul Brand and Philip Yancey, *In His Image* (Grand Rapids, Mich.: Zondervan, 1984), 255, emphasis mine.
10. Zarrow, "Stress: The Facts," *Prevention,* 86.
11. Mara Bovsun, "Young Women At Risk for Heart Disease," UPI. Information from Web site: *www.Applesforhealth.com*, 1:6 (23 July 1999).
12. Michele Hamilton, in the *Los Angeles Times,* on ASH public service Web site.
13. Norma Peterson, "Daily Hassles Are Hazardous," *Reader's Digest* April 1987, 76, emphasis mine.
14. Susan Forward, *Emotional Blackmail* (New York: HarperCollins, 1997), 135–36.

Chapter 8

1. From the article "Job Stress," on *www.stress.org/job.htm*, quoted from The American Institute on Stress.
2. "America's #1 Health Problem," from *www.stress.org/job.htm*, research and quotes provided by the American Institute on Stress.

3. Faith Popcorn, *Dictionary of the Future* (New York: Hyperion, 2001), 78.

4. Charles R. Swindoll, *Stress Fractures* (Sisters, Ore.: Multnomah, 1990), 155, emphasis mine.

5. Ibid.

6. John Eldredge, *Wild At Heart* (Nashville: Thomas Nelson, 2001), 17, emphasis mine.

7. Betty Cuniberti, "Are Working Mothers Really Pioneers?" in *The Courier-Journal* (16 Aug. 1987), H6.

8. Diane Passno, *Feminism: Mystique or Mistake?* (Wheaton, Ill.: Tyndale House, 2000), 118.

9. Karl Menninger, *Whatever Became of Sin?* (New York: Hawthorn Books, Inc., 1973), 91, emphasis mine.

10. Susan Zarrow, "Stress: The Facts," *Prevention* magazine, 39:9, Sept. 1987, 86.

11. Faith Popcorn, *Dictionary of the Future*, 56.

12. George Barna and Mark Hatch, *Boiling Point* (Ventura, Calif.: Regal, 2000), quote taken from Barna's online Web page.

13. Ibid.

14. Arthur Gish, *Beyond the Rat Race* (Scottsdale, Penn.: Herald Press, 1973), 20.

Chapter 9

1. "Rescue Me, Elmo" from Crime Blotter, ABCNEWS.COM, compiled by Oliver Libaw, Sept. 5, 2001, online.

2. Thaddeus Barnum, *Where Is God in Suffering and Tragedy?* (DeBary, Fla.: Longwood Communications, 1997), 13.

3. John Ortberg, *The Life You've Always Wanted* (Grand Rapids, Mich.: Zondervan, 1997), 85.

4. Quoted from John Ortberg, *The Life You've Always Wanted,* 83–84.

5. Lewis B. Smedes, *Shame and Grace* (New York: HarperCollins, 1993), 39.

6. Information from Charles Colson, *BreakPoint,* "Beauty by Syringe—Image Over Character," June 10, 2002, from *BreakPoint* online, a ministry of Prison Fellowship Ministries.

7. Serena Gordon, HealthScoutNews, Feb. 11, online.

8. Caleb Stegall, "Opening Saint Exupery's Box," *Touchstone* (March 2002), 18.

9. Dallas Willard, *The Divine Conspiracy* (San Francisco: HarperSanFrancisco, 1998), 206.

10. Chuck Colson, *Answers to Your Kids' Questions* (Wheaton, Ill.: Tyndale House Publishers, 2000), 191.

11. Bruce Wilkinson, *Secrets of the Vine* (Sisters, Ore.: Multnomah, 2001), 82.

12. Joseph F. Girzone, *Never Alone* (New York: Doubleday, 1994), 98, emphasis mine.

13. John Michael Talbot with Steve Rabey, *The Lessons of St. Francis* (New York: Penguin Group, 1997), 1.

14. Vernard Eller, *The Simple Life* (Grand Rapids, Mich.: William B. Eerdmans Publishing Co., 1973), 122.

15. Guy de Maupassant, *Short Stories of de Maupassant* (Garden City, N.Y.: International Collectors Library, n.d.), 9–16.

16. Richard J. Foster, *Prayer: Finding the Heart's True Home* (San Francisco: HarperSanFrancisco, 1992), 63.

17. Eller, *The Simple Life,* 114.

18. Betsy Hart, "Innocence Goes Belly Up," *The Atlanta Journal-Constitution* (6/18/02), *www.ajc.com online.*

19. Charles Colson, "From Diapers to Thongs: Abercrombie and Outrageous Times," *BreakPoint* Commentary #020617, 06/17/2002.

20. Os Guinness, quoted from Charles Colson, "From Diapers to Thongs: Abercrombie and Outrageous Times."

21. David Elkind, *The Hurried Child: Growing Up Too Fast Too Soon* (Boston: Addison-Wesley Publishing Co., 1981), xii.

22. Frederick C. Van Tatenhove, *Ambition: Friend or Enemy?* (Philadelphia: The Westminster Press, 1984), 36.

23. John Michael Talbot with Steve Rabey, *The Lessons of St. Francis,* 21.

24. Richard Carlson, *Don't Sweat the Small Stuff* (Thorndike, Maine: G. Hall & Co., 1997), 60.

25. Karl Rahner, quoted in Richard J. Foster and Emilie Griffin, *Spiritual Classics* (San Francisco: HarperSanFrancisco, 2000), 218.

Chapter 10

1. Albert L. Meiburg, *Sound Body, Sound Mind* (Philadelphia: The Westminster Press, 1984), 66.

2. Henry David Thoreau, *Walden and Other Writings* (New York: Bantam Books, 1989 [first printing 1854]), 172.

3. Ibid., 174.

4. David McCasland, *Oswald Chambers: Abandoned to God* (Grand Rapids, Mich.: Discovery House, 1993), 63.

5. Emilie Barnes, *The Spirit of Loveliness* (Eugene, Ore.: Harvest House, 1992), 90.

6. Ibid., 91.

7. Henri J. M. Nouwen, *Making All Things New* (New York: Phoenix Press, Walker and Company, 1981), 79–80.

8. Frederick C. Van Tatenhove, *Ambition: Friend or Enemy?* (Philadelphia: The Westminster Press, 1984), 45.

9. David McCasland, *Oswald Chambers: Abandoned to God,* 206.

10. Leith Anderson, *Becoming Friends With God* (Minneapolis: Bethany House, 2001), 230.

11. Quoted from Denise George, *The Christian As a Consumer* (Philadelphia: The Westminster Press, 1984), 26.

12. Richard Carlson, *Don't Sweat the Small Stuff,* 161.

13. Alistair Begg, *The Hand of God* (Chicago: Moody Press, 1999), 195.

14. Information from "The Dangers of Cigarette Smoking," *www.MayoClinic.com,* Nov. 8, 2000.

15. Information quoted from "Smoking Even Worse Than Thought," MSNBC Health, June 19, 2002, online.

16. Greg Winter, "Jury Awards $5.5 Million in a Secondhand Smoke Case," *The New York Times,* online, June 20, 2002.

17. Susan Forward, *Emotional Blackmail* (New York: HarperCollins, 1997), 167.

18. Mara Bovsun, "Young Women At Risk for Heart Disease," United Press International, Vol. 1, Number 6, July 23, 1999, from Applesforhealth.com.

19. Laura Lane, "Walking Reduces Women's Heart Attack Risk," Aug. 25, 1999, quoted from WebMD online.

20. Sheryl Gay Stolberg, "Stress Management for Kindergartners,"

The New York Times online, June 18, 2002.

21. Quoted from Marsha Walton on CNN Sci-Tech, "Salamander Stress Spotted," Cable News Network, May 2, 2002.

22. Meiburg, *Sound Body, Sound Mind*, 65.

23. Wayne E. Oates, *Managing Your Stress* (Indianapolis: Bierce Associates, Inc., 1983), 27.

24. Ibid., 33.

25. Richard Carlson, *Don't Sweat the Small Stuff*, 30.

26. Elaine St. James, *Inner Simplicity* (New York: Hyperion, 1995), 32.

27. David Elkind, *The Hurried Child*, xii, quoted in Frederick C. Van Tatenhove, *Ambition: Friend or Enemy?*, 34.

28. Frederick C. Van Tatenhove, *Ambition: Friend or Enemy?*, 36.

29. Marilyn Chandler McEntyre, "The Fullness of Time," *Christianity Today* online, posted 10/12/00.

30. Elaine St. James, *Inner Simplicity*, 20.

31. See also Denise George and Steven C. Carreker, *Faith for Everyday Stress* (Nashville: Broadman and Holman, 1988), 77.

Chapter 11

1. Thomas Szasz, *The Second Sin*, quoted in Doris Grumbach, *Fifty Days of Solitude* (Rockland, Mass.: Wheeler Publishing, Inc., 1994), 15.

2. Wayne E. Oates, *Managing Your Stress* (Indianapolis: Bierce Associates, Inc., 1983), 62.

3. From *Eaton's Bible Dictionary*, quoted from *Christianity Today* online reference tools.

4. Ibid.

5. Broom tree information from *Holman Concise Bible Dictionary* (Nashville: Broadman & Holman, 1997), 526.

6. Jill Briscoe, *Prayer That Works* (Wheaton, Ill.: Tyndale House, 2000), 136.

Chapter 12

1. David Hansen, *A Little Handbook on Having a Soul* (Downers Grove, Ill.: InterVarsity Press, 1997), 46–48.

2. James M. Freeman, *Manners & Customs of the Bible* (New Kensington, Penn.: Whitaker House, 1996), 317.

3. Matthew Henry, *Matthew Henry's Commentary* on Matthew 11:28, from *Christianity Today* online.

4. Joseph Cardinal Bernardin, *The Journey to Peace* (New York: Doubleday, 2001), 63.

5. Leonard Sweet, *The Jesus Prescription for a Healthy Life* (Nashville: Abington, 1996), 147.

6. "Courting Trouble," *Modern Maturity Magazine,* AARP, July/August 2002, 23.

7. "Navigator," *Modern Maturity Magazine,* AARP, July/August 2002, 23.

Chapter 13

1. Quoted from Gerald Austin, Sr., "Who Is My Neighbor?" in Timothy George and Robert Smith, Jr., *A Mighty Long Journey: Reflections on Racial Reconciliation* (Nashville: Broadman & Holman, 2000), 90.

2. Don M. Aycock, *Be Still and Know* (Nashville: Broadman & Holman, 1999), 66–67.

3. Quote, plus four basic points (explanations mine), taken from Gerald Austin, Sr., "Who Is My Neighbor?" in Timothy George and Robert Smith Jr., *A Mighty Long Journey: Reflections on Racial Reconciliation,* 95.

4. James M. Freeman, *Manners & Customs of the Bible* (New Kensington, Penn.: Whitaker House, 1996), 419.

5. C. S. Lewis, *The Four Loves* (New York: Phoenix Press, 1960), 190.

6. Heather Mercer and Dayna Curry, *Prisoners of Hope* (New York: Doubleday, 2002), 19.

7. Ibid., 212.

8. Forrest Carter, *The Education of Little Tree* (Albuquerque, N.M.: University of New Mexico Press, twenty-fifth anniversary edition, Sept. 2001), selected pages throughout book.

9. Theodore Taylor, *The Cay* (New York: Avon Books, 1969), 111–14.

10. Ibid., 120.

11. C. S. Lewis, *The Four Loves,* 180.

12. David Abel, "A Labor of Love Is Rewarded," *The Boston Globe* online, June 8, 2002, B1.

13. "Chicago man credited with sending thousands to college," *The Associated Press* online, posted Oct. 23, 2001.

14. Information from *www.cnn.com*, "Hate crime reports up in wake of terrorist attacks," Sept. 17, 2001.

15. Paul Brand and Philip Yancey, *In His Image* (Grand Rapids, Mich.: Zondervan, 1984), 247.

16. With the exception of the Brand/Yancey quote, this information on Gandhi came from *www.mkgandhi-sarvodaya.org/index.html*; Indian Gandhian Charitable Institution, Bombay Sarvodaya Mandal (Gandhi Book Center), online.

17. Dolphus Weary story and quotes from Edward Gilbreath, "Catching Up With a Dream, *Christianity Today* "Classic": *www.christianitytoday.com/ct/2000/103/15.0.html*

Chapter 14

1. Read Simon Wiesenthal's story in *The Sunflower: On the Possibilities and Limits of Forgiveness*; story and quotes taken from L. Gregory Jones, reviewer, "Stumped by Repentance," *Christianity Today*, Oct. 26, 1998, Vol. 42, No. 12, 94.

2. Gary Thomas, "The Forgiveness Factor," *Christianity Today,* online, formerly printed in *CT* on Jan. 10, 2000, Vol. 44, No. 1, 38.

3. Ibid., 38.

4. Names have been changed; Kari Schneider's story was written by Kathy Pierce in "The Power of Forgiveness," *Today's Christian Woman,* Sept./Oct. 2000, Vol. 22, No. 5, 78.

5. Mother Teresa, *No Greater Love,* quoted by Richard A. Kauffman, ChristianityToday.com. Posted 1/25/01.

6. George Herbert, quoted in N. T. Wright, *The Lord and His Prayer,* quoted by Richard A. Kauffman, *www.Christianity Today.com.* Posted 1/25/01.

7. Gustavo Gutierrez, *We Drink From Our Own Wells,* quoted by Richard A. Kauffman, *www.ChristianityToday.com.* Posted 1/25/01.

8. Quoted by Lewis B. Smedes, "Keys to Forgiving," *www.ChristianityToday.com*, Dec. 3, 2001.

9. Philip Yancey, *Soul Survivor* (New York: Doubleday, 2001), 214.

10. Henri J. M. Nouwen, *The Wounded Healer* (New York: Imagine Books, 1972), 41.

11. Paul Brand and Philip Yancey, *In His Image* (Grand Rapids, Mich.: Zondervan, 1984), 33.

Chapter 15

1. Brother Lawrence, *The Practice of the Presence of God* (Springdale, Penn.: Whitaker House, 1982), from the cover.

2. Ibid., 33.

3. Ibid., 46.

4. W. A. Criswell, *Why I Preach That the Bible Is Literally True,* reprinted in *The Library of Baptist Classics,* Timothy and Denise George, eds. (Nashville: Broadman & Holman, 1995), summary from selected pages throughout book.

5. Mother Teresa, *In the Heart of the World* (Novato, Calif.: New World Library, 1997), 20.

6. Robert Lawrence Smith, *A Quaker Book of Wisdom* (New York: Eagle Brook, 1998), 2.

7. John Michael Talbot with Steve Rabey, *The Lessons of St. Francis* (New York: Penguin Group, 1997), 59.

8. Thomas Merton, *New Seeds of Contemplation* (New York: New Directions, 1961), 82–83.

9. Oswald Chambers, "After Surrender—What?" in *My Utmost for His Highest* (Uhrichsville, Ohio: Barbour, 1935; 1963), entry from September 13.

10. Gigi Graham Tchividjian and Ruth Bell Graham, *A Quiet Knowing* (Nashville: W Publishing Group, 2001), 5, 7.

11. William V. Pietsch, *The Serenity Prayer Book* (San Francisco: HarperSanFrancisco, 1990), 9.

12. Anna Quindlen, *A Short Guide to a Happy Life* (New York: Random House, 2000), 16–20.

13. Brother Lawrence, *The Practice of the Presence of God,* 33.

14. Catherine Marshall, *Adventures in Prayer* (Grand Rapids, Mich.: Chosen Books, 1975), 65.

15. Hank Hanegraaff, *The Prayer of Jesus,* as quoted from Rhonda Porter Delph, "Rest is not a four-letter Word," *Homelife Magazine* July 2002, 34.

16. William V. Pietsch, *The Serenity Prayer Book,* 57.

Chapter 16

1. Dallas Willard, *The Divine Conspiracy* (San Francisco: Harper-SanFrancisco, 1998), 357.
2. Ibid.
3. Mother Teresa, *In the Heart of the World* (Novato, Calif.: New World Library, 1997), 19.
4. Frederica Mathewes-Green, "A Daily Repentance Workout," *Christianity Today* online, Feb. 4, 2002.
5. Normajean Hinders, *Seasons of a Woman's Life* (Nashville: Broadman & Holman, 1994), 26.
6. Henri J. M. Nouwen, *The Wounded Healer* (New York: Image Books, 1972), 91.
7. Frederica Mathewes-Green, "A Daily Repentance Workout."
8. Martin Luther, quoted from Alistair Begg, *The Hand of God* (Chicago, Ill.: Moody Press, 1999), 186.
9. Charles Swindoll, *Simple Faith* (Dallas: Word, 1991), 128.
10. Leith Anderson, *Becoming Friends With God* (Minneapolis: Bethany House, 2001), 246–47.
11. T. W. Hunt and Melana Hunt Monroe, *From Heaven's View* (Nashville: Broadman & Holman, 2002), 22.
12. Richard J. Foster, *Prayer: Finding the Heart's True Home* (San Francisco: HarperSanFrancisco, 1992), 101.
13. Madame Jeanne Guyon, quoted from ibid., 93.

Postscript and Acknowledgments

A Final Word to the Reader

Dear Reader:

I must admit to you that the year in which I wrote this book—July 1, 2001-July 4, 2002—has been one of the most stressful and unsettling years of my entire life! Not only have I agonized with the rest of the nation regarding the murderous terrorism that has shocked and saddened the United States, but I have agonized over personal and family situations as well. Everywhere I have turned during these twelve months of laborious writing, I have encountered confusion and chaos. I almost hated to admit to my friends that I was trying to write a book on "quiet, solitude, and rest." They just looked at me and knowingly smiled.

It was during this year, and the writing of this book, that God taught me two important lessons about himself and about "quiet, solitude, and rest." First, He showed me that He does, indeed, have a sense of humor. "How can you write about quiet and solitude and rest when you are constantly surrounded by chaos, noise, and confusion?!" my friends have asked me.

Second, God taught me that most women today *live* in chaos, noise, and confusion! He told me to write this book *not* to those who have ample time to rest and pray. He said, "Denise, write this book for women who don't have time to rest, women who must pray hurried prayers, women with overwhelming responsibilities, women with tired brains and stress-broken backs—women who take quick hot showers, not women who soak in warm bubble baths."

"Denise," He convinced me by allowing me untold crises every day of this whole past year, "women in this busy society can't always (if ever) 'escape' into restful solitude when they get tired. Women today work demanding jobs, rear energetic children, help busy husbands, keep house, mow yards, and unstop toilets. I am calling them to the Quiet, but you must show them where the Quiet Place is. Tell them for Me that within each woman's heart dwells the Quiet Place. Tell them I am waiting for them to come, that I am extending my comforting shoulder to them, that I want to renew their minds, strengthen their bodies, and refresh their tired hearts.

"Tell them, Denise! Tell them that life is more like a busy Jackson, Tennessee, waffle house than a peaceful monastery on a Swiss mountaintop."

So, dear readers, this is His message through me to you. Believe me, the practical suggestions I offer within the pages of this book do work: I have practiced them myself for the past 367 days! I must confess to you, I am glad to be writing these final words. I have painfully *lived* this book—its pages are stained with my sweat and my tears. Even today, July 4, 2002, as I type these last words, I am hearing on television news that several people have just been shot and killed at the El Al ticket counter at the Los Angeles airport—the same airline I flew recently to the Middle East.

I can tell you from firsthand experience that, within the chaos and confusion and conflict of Earth-life, it is God himself who waits within the chapel of our heart's Quiet Place to take you and me into His loving arms and offer us His divine rest. How beautiful are His words to me right now: "Come to Me, all you who labor and are heavy laden, and I will give you rest."

Thank you, Lord.

My heartfelt thank-you to all the wonderful people who helped me to make it through this year and who helped me in the writing of this book: my editor, Steve Laube; my literary agent, Greg Johnson; and my dear friend and literary mentor, Dr. Calvin Miller.

Thank you

- to my supporting and loving friends Doris Hughston, Pat Batson, Sandy Luster, Carolyn Tomlin, Maurreen Salter, the Reverend Roger Salter, Dr. Bill O'Brien, Dr. Dellanna O'Brien, Dr. Robert Smith, Jr., Jim Cox, Dr. T. W. Hunt, and many others;
- to the faculty, staff, and students of Beeson Divinity School, Samford University, Birmingham, Alabama, for your love, encouragement, and theological instruction;
- to the members of the St. Matthews Episcopal Church for your gracious welcome and kindness to me this year;
- to my wonderful mother, Willene Williams Wyse, to my sister, Jill Marie Wyse, and to a person who has become like a second father to me: Oscar S. Hilliard.

A special thank-you to my family—my husband of thirty-two years, Dr. Timothy George, and to my children, Christian Timothy and Alyce Elizabeth. I love you and I appreciate you.

And thank you, Lord, for your loving closeness to me as I have struggled to speak to women who yearn, like I do, for your strong, supporting shoulder in the solitude and rest of the Quiet.

Prepare to Encounter God

A WOMAN'S GUIDE TO PERSONAL RETREAT

The point of a spiritual retreat has always been to escape into the calm arms of God. This book leads you into that meaningful time with God—whether your retreat is your daily quiet time or a day or two getaway.

Quiet Places by Jane Rubietta

PURSUE STILLNESS AS A WAY OF LIFE

Do you walk through the responsibilities of your life with an inner peace, confidence, and conviction? Or do you barrel through with a harried, frazzled, and disorganized approach? This book will help you stop the crisis-dodging life as you are encouraged and enabled to embrace stillness in the Lord as a lifestyle. You will learn to recognize your own spiritual inattentiveness, to be content with how God designed you, to be confident in God-given wisdom, and finally to trust God's personal faithfulness in your life. *Be Still* by Elizabeth Hoekstra